LAO TZU AND ANTHROPOSOPHY

ALSO BY KWAN-YUK CLAIRE SIT

The Lord's Prayer: An Eastern Perspective

LAO TZU
and
ANTHROPOSOPHY

A Translation of the *Tao Te Ching*
with Commentary and a Lao Tzu Document
"The Great One Excretes Water"

Kwan-Yuk Claire Sit
薛羅君鈺

Lindisfarne Books
2010

2010
Lindisfarne Books
An imprint of SteinerBooks, Inc.
610 Main Street, Great Barrington, MA 01230
www.steinerbooks.org

Cover art copyright © by Kit-Keung Kan, *Falling Water XXVI*, 2009,
Chinese ink and watercolor on rice paper, 38" x 36" (96.5 cm x 91.5 cm)
Author photo copyright © by Emil Sit, 2008
Book and cover design by Jens Jensen

LIBRARY OF CONGRESS CATALOGING-IN-PUBLICATION DATA
Laozi.
   [Dao de jing. English]
   Lao Tzu and Anthroposophy : a translation of the Tao te ching with
commentary and a Lao Tzu document "The great one excretes water" /
[edited by] Kwan-Yuk Claire Sit.
      p. cm.
   Includes bibliographical references and index.
   ISBN 978-1-58420-087-1
   1. Laozi. Dao de jing. 2. Taoism—Relations—Anthroposophy.
3. Anthroposophy—Relations—Taoism. I. Sit, Kwan-Yuk C. II. Taiyi
sheng shui. English. III. Title. IV. Title: Great one excretes water.
   BL1900.L26E5 2010
   299.5'1482—dc22
                                                      2010022521

Printed in the United States of America

CONTENTS

PREFACE

An author once quipped that there may be more writers who translate and comment on the *Tao Te Ching* (also known as the *Lao Tzu*) than there are readers. This is probably an overstatement, and yet we cannot deny that this masterpiece by Lao Tzu is exceedingly popular. The *Tao Te Ching* no doubt reveals profound universal truths and instills an intimate enchantment in its readers. Although many have explored it extensively, some still find uncharted areas pertaining to their own particular interests. I am one such reader-turned-writer who is enthusiastic about sharing her investigation with readers of this classic.

The subject of *Tao* is so vast and comprises such a wide array of attributes that no one book could ever exhaust it. Each book can deal with only particular aspects of *Tao*. The present book, probing the *Lao Tzu* with the teachings of Anthroposophy,[1] is intended for those who yearn for a life of harmonized spirituality and practicality.

My initial reading of the *Lao Tzu*, twenty some years ago, was very superficial. My knowledge of classical Chinese (*wen-yan-wen* 文言文) was inadequate to understand this work. To learn what it is about, I had to rely on the accompanying notes and commentaries written in contemporary Chinese (*bai-hua-wen* 白話文). I skimmed the book and found many useful aphorisms. I was also intrigued by its heavy use of oxymora. At the time, I did not ponder their deeper meanings and was keen to move on to other subjects.

---

1   See appendix 1 for a brief introduction to Anthroposophy.

When working on the manuscript of my book *The Lord's Prayer*, I reread the *Lao Tzu* to incorporate some of its sayings. I was also studying Anthroposophy and practicing an exercise recommended by the original teacher of Anthroposophy, Rudolf Steiner (1861–1925). In this exercise, I tried to recall, in reverse, subject matter I encountered—poems, stories, events, and so on. After succeeding in reciting some short Tang poems in reverse, I naively challenged myself to tackle chapters of the *Tao Te Ching*. To my surprise, I could hardly recall the chapters in normal order, let alone recite them in reverse. It was very frustrating that their details kept slipping through my mind. At last it dawned on me that this inability to recall them was because of my lack of true comprehension of the material. Hence, I committed myself to studying the *Lao Tzu* scrupulously. It is both amazing and gratifying that my interest in Anthroposophy has been instrumental in enhancing my cognition of this deeply veiled classic.

According to Steiner, human consciousness evolves over long eons. We started with a dim, trance-like consciousness, which developed gradually to a clear, wakeful consciousness. It has taken humankind many millennia to progress from sentience, to intellect, to self-awareness. Before (and even during) the development of sentient consciousness, human beings had a kind of dreamy consciousness and were vaguely aware of their connection with the spiritual world. They could perceive messages of the "gods" through oracles or divination of special signs in nature. "Mystery centers" existed where advanced teachers trained initiates to perceive and understand the gods' mandates. Those initiates would then use their perceived knowledge to assist in governing. These were highly disciplined individuals who had deep compassion toward others and would not succumb to material temptations. In his teachings, Steiner deals mainly with the Western esoteric tradition, but he also indicates that guidance by the spiritual world in ancient times was universal. Thus, I surmise that the ancient Taoist masters in China played roles similar to those of Western initiates.

Anthroposophy teaches that human beings are meant to develop the intellectual mind, through which we can make moral judgments freely on our own (see appendix 1). Direct guidance from the spiritual world slowly diminished, and the spiritual world, or *Tao,* is far less involved in guiding human affairs. It has receded and become hidden deeply within each human being as one's conscience. This hidden aspect of *Tao* is probably what Taoists refer to as the "real being"; what Buddhists call Buddha nature, or the Cosmic Buddha; and what Christians identify as the Christ or Holy Spirit. Steiner explains that outside guidance has slowly ebbed over the span of many millennia. Even in this modern age, a faint remnant of the initiate tradition still exists in remote corners of the world. I speculate that the stories of Carlos Castaneda (1925–1998) recount his initiation experience with the shaman Don Juan of a certain decadent Indian tradition.[2]

During Lao Tzu's time, Taoists no longer engaged directly in the affairs of the government and played only an obscure role in society. What the remote past had been and what disappeared in later times is clearly indicated in the *Tao Te Ching* by certain statements: "Taoist adepts of old..." (chapter 15); "Therefore, when the Great Tao recedes..." (chapter 18); "Of old, these attained oneness..." (chapter 39); "Why did the ancients value this *Tao* so much..." (chapter 62); "The ancients who practiced *Tao*..." (chapter 65); "This is known as matching Heaven—the ultimate of the ancients..." (chapter 68); and so on.

Since outside guidance has receded, it is vital that we learn to pay attention to the inner prompting of *Tao.* We train our minds so that we can "attain emptiness to the far end" and "keep stillness in the deep bottom" (chapter 16). When we engage in chasing after fame and wealth, we

---

2   Cf. http://en.wikipedia.org/wiki/Carlos_Castaneda (09/26/10).

unwittingly excite the mind. Therefore we must make conscientious and diligent efforts to "disregard the without and take care of the within" (chapter 12). In fact, in discerning the hidden *Tao*, "the further one goes out, the less one knows" (chapter 47). This shift of guidance by *Tao* from the outer to the inner inevitably created a few problems in the transition.

Let us consider several issues during the time of Lao Tzu. First, because the ruling elite governed their nation without the wise guidance of Taoists, they easily fell into traps of human follies, created commotion in society, and caused people great suffering (chapters 72, 75). Lao Tzu's frequent mention of how the rulers of antiquity maintained an orderly society reflects his concern over the unruliness of the nations at his time (chapters 17, 39, 57, 65).

Second, the number of students willing to study and follow Taoist tradition must have been declining, since the practice of *Tao* was no longer a vehicle to prominent government positions. It is no wonder that Lao Tzu laments that "they do not care to know me. Those who know me are few. Those who follow me are even rarer" (chapter 70).

Third, most Taoist masters probably maintain a very low profile, or even "remain hidden" (chapter 15). Hence, when individuals do wish to study Taoism, they may have difficulty finding a genuine teacher. Books such as the *Tao Te Ching* can fill the gap somewhat, but books are not ideal teachers. Certain esoteric practices require not only oral instruction from a teacher, but also a teacher's assurance of the student's unselfish and humble character. Nonetheless, a well-conceived book can still inspire.

It was probably within the context of such a historical background that Lao Tzu compiled the oral Taoist tradition and wrote the *Tao Te Ching*. Yet, we do not really know who Lao Tzu was. The traditional view maintains that the author Lao Tzu can be any one of three persons. One is Li Er 李耳, whom Confucius (551–479 B.C.E.) had visited. Another is Lao Lai Tzu 老萊子, another contemporary of Confucius. The third is Lao Dan 老儋,

who once had an audience with Duke Xian 獻公 of Qin (r. 384–362 B.C.E.).[3] Some scholars opine that the *Tao Te Ching* is a work of the Warring Period (404–221 B.C.E.). If so, then the author referred to as Lao Tzu could not have been a contemporary of Confucius. Whatever the case, we do not need to know who Lao Tzu was to reap the benefits of his profound teaching.

In the *Tao Te Ching*, Lao Tzu frequently indicates how the sage leads the people and says; "In the realm there are four greats, and the king is one of them" (chapter 25). It seems as if the *Tao Te Ching* is a book for teaching kings and lords how to rule. When we understand that the word *king* is meant to represent the ideal human being—one who can be a role model leading others—we realize that Lao Tzu is actually teaching individuals to become "sage kings," or simply "sages."[4] Essentially, he is showing readers a path to self-realization.

The *Tao Te Ching* is divided into two parts. In part one, the "Tao Ching," or "Book of Tao," Lao Tzu explores the universal principle of *Tao*. In part two, the "Te Ching," or "Book of Te," he provides practical advice on how to actualize the virtues of *Tao*. Ingeniously, he uses the affairs of worldly kings to illustrate the conduct of the ideal human being. He is not necessarily guiding secular kings to rule states, though his teaching is surely applicable in this respect and would certainly benefit those rulers who followed it. More to the point, he shows people how to rule the state of their own self.

We reason that Lao Tzu is perhaps writing for the common people, because he often uses ordinary objects and activities to shed light on the deep and subtle aspects of *Tao*. War was rampant during his time, and he had keen empathy for the anguish of people during such times (see chapters 30, 31, 80). Thus it is natural for him to point out the inhuman aspects of

---

3   Cf. http://en.wikipedia.org/wiki/Laozi (09/26/2010).

4   See comments in chapter 25.

war and to explore ways of minimizing battle causalities. He sighs, "Since so many are killed, it is befitting to be mournful and tearful; even a victory should be observed as a funeral" (chapter 31). He is wholeheartedly a peace-loving man. He advocates negotiations over battles: "Those who are good accomplish only their mission. They do not triumph by force.... If they have no option to succeed, they abide" (chapter 30). If war is utterly unavoidable, he stresses treating the opponent with compassion: "Indeed, compassion enables you to win in battles and be secure in defense. It is as if Heaven keeps what it would establish within a wall of compassion" (chapter 67).

Until 1973, there were only a few traditional editions of the *Lao Tzu* without significant differences. One of the more popular among those editions is often called the Wang Bi (WB 王弼) edition. Readers associate his name with this popular edition Wang Bi (226–249), because he was the first scholar to comment in a systematic way on the *Lao Tzu* from a philosophical perspective. To learn about Wang's comments, readers may consult, for example, *The Classic of the Way and Virtue* by Richard John Lynn.

Then, in 1973, archeologists found two copies of the *Lao Tzu* among a library of literary classics in a tomb from around 168 B.C.E. at Mawangdui (MWD 馬王堆) in the city of Changsha, Hunan Province.[5] While the Chinese call these two copies the "Silk Scripted Lao Tzu," Western scholars generally refer to them as the "MWD text."

Later, in 1993, archeologists found another collection of *Lao Tzu* documents in a tomb dated before 278 B.C.E. at Guodian 郭店, Hubei Province.[6] This collection is referred to as the "Bamboo Slip Lao Tzu." We have translated and commented on two items from this collection (see chapter 63 and appendix 2). At this point we will focus on the MWD text and contrast it with the WB edition.

---

5   See Henricks, *Lao-Tzu Te-Tao Ching*, pp. xii–xiv.

6   See Henricks, *Lao Tzu's Tao Te Ching*, pp. 1–8.

The two MWD copies (referred to as Text A and Text B) are written on silk in script styles no longer in common use. Judging from the script and the use of taboo words, scholars infer that Text A was copied some time before the reign of the first Han Dynasty emperor, Liu Pang 劉邦 (r. 206–194 B.C.E.), whereas Text B was copied during his reign.[7] The content of these two copies are essentially identical, with only minor differences in wording. Though there are missing words in both copies (sometimes quite extensively in Text A), one can, with reference to the traditional editions, render the "Silk Scripted Lao Tzu" a comprehensive text.

The texts of the MWD and the WB are also essentially the same. They differ significantly, however, in the arrangement of the content and subtly in some wording. Let us outline their differences and show how we synthesize them in this book.

In the WB edition the text is divided into eighty-one numbered chapters. The beginning chapters (1–37) are called the "Tao Ching" and the remaining chapters (38–81) the "Te Ching." By contrast, the MWD text has no chapter divisions, but only a clear separation into two parts. For convenience, we use the WB chapter numbers when referring to the MWD text. In the MWD text, the order of the "Tao Ching" and the "Te Ching" are reversed; part one is the "Te Ching" and part two the "Tao Ching." Yet, within each part, the chapter sequences of the MWD are almost identical to that of the WB except for three deviations. Specifically, 24 is placed between 21 and 22; 41 is placed between 39 and 40; and 80 and 81 are placed between 66 and 67 (see the following chapter lists).

My reading of both versions convinces me that the "Tao Ching" should nonetheless come before the "Te Ching." Consequently, I follow the WB presentation of the two parts. However, within each part the arrangement of the chapters in the MWD text is definitely more coherent than that of

---

7   See Henricks, *Lao-Tzu Te-Tao Ching*, p. xv.

the WB edition. Hence, within each part, I adopt the MWD order except chapter 41, which I place between 38 and 39 instead of between 39 and 40. Please refer to the relevant chapters for the reason of these juxtapositions. To show how the arrangement of this book differs from that of the WB and the MWD, we list the chapter orders below:

WB:

Book One: Tao Ching

1, 2–21, 22, 23, 24, 25–36, 37

Book Two: Te Ching

38, 39, 40, 41, 42–66, 67–78, 79, 80, 81

MWD:

Book One: Te Ching

38, 39, 40, (41), 42–66, 67–78, 79, (80, 81)

Book Two: Tao Ching

1, 2–21, 22, 23, (24), 25–36, 37

This book:

Book One: Tao Ching

1, 2–21, 22, 23, (24), 25–36, 37

Book Two: Te Ching

38, 39, 40, (41), 42–66, 67–78, 79, (80, 81)

Let us now examine the differences in wording. With reference to the WB edition, we find that here and there in the MWD text, a long clause or a few words are added, left out, or changed. Readers interested in a detailed (word-by-word) comparison between these two versions may consult works by D. C. Lau, *Tao Te Ching* and Henricks, *Lao-Tzu Te-Tao Ching*. It is interesting that the MWD text is generally more revealing of Lao Tzu's ideas. It may not have brought about a revolutionary perspective of the *Tao Te Ching,* but the MWD text definitely presents a more penetrating reading of this classic. Indeed, experts are still conducting in-depth research of the MWD text, and we can expect a more insightful reading of the *Lao Tzu* to appear in the near future (see comments in chapter 75).

In this book, although we use the WB edition as a template, we largely adopt the whole MWD text. Many of those adoptions provide a finer nuance in the content, which we deem unnecessary to specify. However, when the MWD and the WB convey significantly different views we will comment on them, and depending on how they differ we may also include both texts for comparison (see e.g. chapters 8 and 20).

When preparing this manuscript, I owe the efforts of many prior translators and commentators of the *Lao Tzu*. Their renditions provide a luxuriant field for me to harvest and greatly enrich my writing experience.

A Special Note on romanization: except for well-known names and terms such as Lao Tzu, Chuang Tzu, and *Tao* (using the Wade-Giles system), most Chinese names and terms are romanized using the pinyin system, the most commonly used for Standard Mandarin.

BOOK ONE
TAO CHING

1

道，可道也，非恆 道也。名，可名也，非恆名也。無，名萬 物之始也；有，名
萬物之母也。故恆無欲也，以觀其妙；恆有欲也，以觀其所徼。兩者同出，異名
同謂。玄之又玄，眾妙之門。

A *Tao* that can be a road is not the eternal *Tao*.
A name that can connote fame is not the eternal Name.
Wu[1] is named for the origin of all things.
You[2] is named for the mother of all things.
So, ever free of desire, we can see its subtleties.
Ever full of desire, we can see only its manifestations.
These two[3] appear together.
They differ in name, yet are considered the same.
Mystery within mystery,
    they are the gateway to all marvels.

COMMENTS

We are embarking on a wonderful journey of the *Tao Te Ching*. The
terms *Tao, wu,* and *you* have very rich connotations that we may not fully
apprehend in the first reading. However, when we keep an open mind and
patiently follow Lao Tzu's guidance, we can gradually deepen our appreciation of their intrigue yet far-reaching implications.

    The word *Tao* (道) can be used as either a verb or a noun. As a verb, it
means to guide or to speak. As a noun, it stands for a road, a guide or method,
or the eternal Way—something that seems to exist, and yet it is so difficult
to grasp that Lao Tzu expounds on it with more than five thousand words.

---

1   *Wu* 無: Non-revealing, non-tangible, or nothingness.

2   *You* 有: Revealing, tangible, or essence.

3   *Wu* 無 and *you* 有.

3

Nam Huai-Jin 南懷瑾 (b. 1918) explains that using the word *Tao* 道 to mean "speak" is quite recent. He says this usage was common during the Tang and Sung dynasties (618–1279), but not during Lao Tzu's time, around the sixth to fourth centuries B.C.E.[4] Hence, we avoid this particular meaning in reading the *Tao Te Ching*.

Tao is also the sound for the Primal Wisdom. Rudolf Steiner relates that "The wisdom of Atlantis was embodied in the water, in a drop of dew. And the word dew [*Tau* in German] is nothing other than the ancient Atlantean sound."[5] Someone has even suggested that Taoism is an offshoot of the long-lost civilization of Atlantis. Nevertheless, we do not need to know about ancient Atlantis to appreciate the sublime wisdom of *Tao*.

In the two opening lines of the *Tao Te Ching*, Lao Tzu is making a pun on the words *Tao* 道 and *ming* 名. *Tao* 道, as a road, can be walked, but not as the Primal Wisdom *Tao*. *Ming*名, which is a name connoting temporary fame, is not the eternal Name of *Tao*. Lao Tzu is setting a tone for his exposition. We shall see that he is fond of using oxymora. For instance, he says, "*Tao* is eternal and nameless" (chapter 32), yet "from the present back to antiquity, its Name has never gone away" (chapter 21). Furthermore, he is also adept at illuminating deep and difficult subjects with simple and common objects. For example, he symbolizes the bestowing virtue of *Tao* by a vessel (chapter 4). His juxtaposition of similar yet different ideas subtly sparks us to ponder seriously his profound messages.

When we use *wu* and *you* to name the non-revealing and revealing attributes of the Primal Wisdom *Tao,* we are actually confining them to something specific, yet they are more than such designations. Names are merely makeshift labels for discussion, not the real thing.

---

4   Nam, *Lao Tzu Ta Shui* 老子他說, p. 36.

5   *The Secret Stream: Christian Rosenkreutz & Rosicrucianism,* p. 36.

Before creation, *Tao* is in the non-revealing state, dark and void. There is no substance in it, yet it is pregnant with potential for everything. This state, which we can consider the origin of all things, is called *wu*. When creating, *Tao* is in the revealing state, manifesting its essence in everything. This state, which we can consider the mother of all things, is called *you*. Herein lies the deep mystery of *Tao*; these two states always appear together and are regarded as one. *Tao* is forever revealing, creating a myriad of things, and simultaneously non-revealing, returning to the void with nothing in it.

We may find it puzzling that a thing is concurrently "being" and "non-being." Maybe the example of a photon in quantum physics can throw light on this mystery. A photon has a wave–particle duality. It can be treated as a particle, yet its wave characteristics can always be calculated. This example is somewhat technical; Lao Tzu offers simpler and more appropriate examples in chapter 11. At present, he simply tells us that *Tao* is in a state of "oneness," eternally creating and disintegrating. We cannot separate the two processes. *Tao* is indeed deep and profound.

If Lao Tzu can discern and inform us in this mystery, then shouldn't we also be able to savor its wonders. He imparts to us an exceedingly powerful practice to gain entry to this mystery within mystery. He advises us to get rid of our desires. He explains that while we are filled with desire we see only the outer manifestations of *Tao*. Only when we are without desire can we know its inner subtleties. The *Tao Te Ching* is essentially a guide on taming desires.

2

天下皆知美之為美，斯惡已；皆知善之為善，斯不善矣。有無相生，難易相成，長短相形，高下相盈，音聲相和，先后相隨，恆也。是以聖人處無為之事，行不言之教，萬物作而弗始，生而弗有，為而弗恃，成功而弗居。夫唯弗居，是以弗去。

Everyone recognizes beauty as beautiful.
This is because there is ugliness.
Everyone recognizes goodness as good.
This is because there is badness.
The have and the have-not produce each other.
The difficult and the easy complete each other.
The long and the short shape each other.
The high and the low fulfill each other.
Tone and sound harmonize each other.[6]
The front and the back follow each other.
They are always so.
Therefore, sages manage affairs with non-action (*wu-wei*)[7]
    and conduct teaching without words.
They let all things arise freely,
    produce without possessiveness,
    act without conceit,
    accomplish without claiming credit.
Because they claim no credit,
    no credits are lost.

---

6   Nowadays, we regard *sound* (*sheng* 聲) and *tone* (*yin* 音) as synonyms. However, in ancient China, the word *sound* refers to a single sound, while *tone* is a mixture of sounds. For a discussion on the difference between the terms *tone* and *sound* in ancient China, see Chen Cheng-Yih, *Early Chinese Work in Natural Science: A Re-examination of the Physics of Motion, Acoustics, Astronomy, and Scientific Thoughts*, pp. 19–20.

7   The term *non-action* (*wu-wei* 無為) does not mean inaction or no action. It refers to the stilled mind that is not stirred by desires. We shall learn more fully the meaning of *non-action* in chapters 43 through 48. For now it suffices to interpret non-action as action without selfish desire.

COMMENTS

Tao is in the state of unity, but we are in its created world of duality. For us, neither goodness nor badness can exist by itself. To discern one, we need the presence of the other as a point of reference. When people differentiate the polarities, they may develop a preference, wanting to keep one or to avoid the other. Yet the two poles are not static. One pole will naturally lead to the other. We can never hold on to or avoid either pole.

Therefore, when the sage manages affairs, the mind is not stirred toward one pole or the other. This state of the mind without desire stirring it is called non-action (*wu-wei*). The sage teaches through exemplifying conduct, letting things arise freely, producing without possessiveness, acting without conceit, claiming no credits for achievements. In fact, credit, like everything else, comes and goes dynamically. By claiming no credits, one loses no credits.

3

不尚賢，使民不爭；不貴難得之貨，使民不為盜；不見可欲，使民不亂。是以聖
人之治也，虛其心，實其腹；弱其志，強其骨。恆使民無知無欲也。使夫知不敢
弗為而已，則無不治。

> Not adulating talents prevents people from contending.
> Not valuing hard-to-get goods prevents people from stealing.
> Not displaying what is desirable prevents people from agitating.
> So that is how the sage governs:
>> empty the mind and fill the belly;[8]
>> weaken the ambition and strengthen the bones.
> Always keep the people from being clever and without desire.[9]
> Make them know to restrain from acting erratically,
>> then everything will be in order.

COMMENTS

This chapter discusses how to rule people. Proper rule is neither for control nor to claim credit, but to lead as a role model. When the ruler does
not act erratically, the nation will follow suit and be orderly. Thus, the
principal criterion for a ruler is the ability to rule one's own self, to tame
desire and to weaken one's ambition. In a broad sense, each person is a
ruler of the self. Thus, this teaching on ruling applies to everyone.

---

8   The "belly" is where the *qi* center is located, about two inches below the navel.
    Taoist tradition holds that filling the belly with *qi* is conducive to longevity. Nev-
    ertheless, we read the *Tao Te Ching* more with a philosophical slant than with
    concern for longevity.

9   "Not being clever" and "without desire" are major themes of the *Tao Te Ching*
    and recur often.

To avoid succumbing to temptations, people need a firm will to keep the mind from becoming agitated. To this end, Lao Tzu advises us to keep the belly filled and the bones strengthened. Let us investigate the wisdom of this suggestion.

Experience indicates that well-fed people are generally more content and less likely to commit crimes. Additionally, we hail those who are not corrupted by temptations as having "strong bones." Thus, we connect the belly and the bones subconsciously with the mind and the will.

Alchemical Taoism may shed light on this advice. Its doctrine uses the trigrams HEAVEN ☰ and EARTH ☷ to symbolize the will and mind in their primal state, and the trigrams WATER ☵ and FIRE ☲ to represent the will and mind in their fettered state.[10] HEAVEN consists of three solid (yang) lines, indicating the leadership strength of the will. EARTH consists of three broken (yin) lines, indicting the mind's virtues of receptivity and submission. FIRE, with the yin line in the middle and two yang lines outside, indicates that the mind is no longer open but filled with desire and ambition to lead. WATER, with the yang line hidden between two yin lines, indicates a will that is weakened by a fettered mind. Symbolically, to empty the mind means to revert the two outer yang lines of FIRE to yin, so the mind is like EARTH, receptive and submitting. To fill the belly and to strengthen the bones mean to revert the two outer yin lines of WATER to yang, so that the will is like HEAVEN, with firm leadership strength.[11]

Anthroposophy can deepen our appreciation of Lao Tzu's suggestion in a different perspective. Steiner teaches that on Earth people function in three domains: thinking, feeling, and willing. He explains that thinking is associated primarily with the head, feeling the rhythmic (lung and

---

10   Cf. Sit, *The Lord's Prayer*, pp. 135–137.

11   See comments in chapter 10.

9

blood) system, and willing the metabolic and limb organization. These three functions subtly affect one another.[12]

On the one hand, thinking that is easily influenced by feelings of likes and dislikes will generate a great array of desire and aversion in one's thoughts. When the mind is empty of such thoughts, we also lessen our ambition. On the other hand, science does not yet know exactly how willing works, but Rudolf Steiner teaches that willing is connected with our metabolic process and the limb movements. When we have eaten and move our limbs, the food is burned up by the metabolic process and helps the will to be reflected as mental images in the mind. Thus, when the mind is not clouded by ambitious thoughts, the belly is filled with food, and the limbs are moved by strong bones, the will not to act erratically becomes clearer in one's thinking. There is indeed great wisdom in the counsel, "Empty the mind and fill up the belly. Weaken the ambition and strengthen the bones."

12   See, for example, Steiner, *The Foundations of Human Experience*, pp. 49ff.

4

道沖，而用之有不盈也。淵兮，似萬物之宗。挫其銳，解其紛，和其光，同其
塵。湛兮，似或存。吾不知其誰之子，象帝之先。

> *Tao* is empty.
> Yet its use is as a bottomless vessel that is inexhaustible.
> Oh, how profound, the apparent source of all things.
> It blunts sharp edges.
> It unravels tangles.
> It softens brightness.
> It merges with dusts.[13]
> Oh, how darkly vague; it seems barely existent.
> I do not know whose child it is.
> Its image precedes the Heavenly Lords.

COMMENTS

The metaphor of *Tao* as an empty, bottomless vessel recalls this fairy tale:

> A poor family has a magic empty bowl. Whenever they need anything
> they take out the bowl and make a wish, and goods appear from it. One
> day, the couple next door discover the family's secret and steal their bowl.
> Being greedy, they keep thinking up wishes for valuable goods. Piles of
> treasure pour from the bowl so quickly that the couple is soon buried
> alive.

Generally, none of us are as greedy as that couple.

Before continuing to chapter 5, let us digress and consider Lao Tzu's
writing style in the *Tao Te Ching*. He structures his work the way a

---

13 *Dust* is a metaphor for the world. "Merging with dusts" means one is not above
the world but is humbly submerged in it. It also symbolizes the sage who is willing
to remain behind in the dusts that are stirred up by the people in the front.

composer scores a piece of music. He announces and explores themes and revisits them with variations in later chapters.

For example, in chapter 1 he announces the main theme on the profound and subtle nature of *Tao*. In chapters 2 and 3, he introduces more themes, stressing the non-possessive aspect of *Tao*. Now he shifts to illumine *Tao*'s marvelous bestowing virtue in chapters 4 to 6. It is a good exercise to detect variations of the announced themes in the later chapters to deepen our appreciation of the *Tao Te Ching*.

We may gradually learn that Lao Tzu often expounds topics in a series of three chapters. Thus, the structure of the *Tao Te Ching* reveals a "signature of three" that illustrates an important characteristic of *Tao* (see chapters 14 and 42).

5

天地不仁，以萬物為芻狗；聖人不仁，以百姓為芻狗。天地之間，其猶橐籥乎？
虛而不屈，動而愈出。多聞數窮，不若守於中。

> Heaven and Earth are not sentimental.
> They regard all things as straw dogs.[14]
> Sages are not sentimental.
> They regard all people as straw dogs.
> Isn't the space between Heaven and Earth like a bellows?
> It is empty yet inexhaustible.
> The harder it moves, the more it produces.
> More listening[15] or frequent probing:
>> neither is as good as staying in the middle.

COMMENTS

Suppose we consider the virtues such as blunting sharp edges, unraveling tangles, softening brightness, and merging with dusts, as the feminine traits of *Tao*. By contrast, we may regard the virtue of being non-sentimental as its masculine trait. Indeed, *Tao* and human beings, as well, are both masculine and feminine. (For discussion on this aspect of men, see chapter 28 and appendix 1.)

In this chapter, we can detect the subtle recurrence of the themes "managing affairs with non-action" and "teaching without words" (chapter

---

14 In ancient times, straw dogs were constructed for ceremonies. One would not attach any sentiment to them, since they are discarded after use.

15 Suppose there are ten possible solutions to a problem. Ideally a good student, after just listening to one solution, would be able to figure out all ten. So there is no need to listen repeatedly. There is a modern Chinese writer whose name is Wen I-duo 聞一多 literally, "Listen, once-many." Probably he deems that listening once is already too many times. Indeed, by stilling our mind we can know what we need to do without listening to other people's suggestion.

2). We may reason that Heaven and Earth teach the sage without words. They show the sage to be unsentimental. Thus the sage can manage affairs through non-action. Not being sentimental, sages do not stir the mind with likes and dislikes. They cling to nothing. No matter what the object is, after it has been used, they will let go of it as they would a straw dog.

Though Heaven and Earth are not sentimental, nature nevertheless provides. Here Lao Tzu uses a bellows to emphasize the miraculous feature of *Tao's* bestowing virtue. It is empty inside, yet it can produce air when operated. The amount of air produced depends on the manner of operation. In fact, the air that blows out is none other than the air drawn in. Thus, if we can keep the mind empty like a bellows (without a myriad of selfish desires), we can accomplish our task exactly as intended.

Lao Tzu illustrates this input-output phenomenon again in the next chapter, and he explores it more fully in chapters 22 to 24. For now, he does not elaborate much.

"More listening or frequent probing: Neither is as good as staying in the middle." The important thing is to maintain the mind like the middle of a bellows—empty of sentiments.

6

谷神不死，是謂玄牝。玄牝之門，是謂天地根。綿綿若存，用之不勤。

> The valley spirit never dies.
> It is called the mystic female.
> The gateway of the mystic female
>   is the root of Heaven and Earth.
> Lingering like a thread, it barely seems to exist.
> Yet its use is inexhaustible.

COMMENTS

A valley is open and spacious. On the one hand it facilitates vapors in rising to Heaven and helps dews condense on the Earth, as though it is the mystic gate between Heaven and Earth. On the other hand, like a responsive female, it always echoes what is sounded. Hence, the spirit of the valley is called the mystic female.

Lao Tzu provides three metaphors illuminating the bestowing virtue of *Tao*: a vessel, a bellows, and a valley. He notes its humble attribute in chapter 4, its unsentimental attribute in chapter 5, and its mystic attribute in this chapter. Yet he keeps one common theme: "It is empty yet inexhaustible."

We may view the valley spirit as a metaphor, but there is no reason to doubt the existence of spirits in nature. For example, there are many stories about Taoists taming evil spirits by charms and talismans. In more modern times, Rudolf Steiner explains the functions of elemental spirits in many of his anthroposophic lectures.[16]

The Taoist tradition considers the human body a microcosm of *Tao*. Thus, every man has a "mystic female" within. Finding it, one

---

16   For references, see Smith, *The Burning Bush*, pp. 561–564.

automatically has access to the root of Heaven and Earth or a way to longevity. Some Taoists assert that chapter 16 actually teaches how to get to the root of Heaven and Earth. However, as stated earlier (see note 8, page 8), this study of the *Tao Te Ching* is not intended for longevity but for a more meaningful and fulfilling life.

7

天長地久。天地之所以能長且久者，以其不自生，故能長生。是以聖人後其身而
身先，外其身而身存。不以其無私邪？故能成其私。

> Heaven lasts and Earth endures.
> Why do Heaven last and Earth endure?
> It is because they do not exist for themselves.
> Therefore, they can be ever-living.
> Hence, sages remain behind yet lead.
> They detach themselves from safety yet endure.
> Is it not because they are selfless that they are self-realized?

COMMENTS

Lao Tzu talks about the never-dying mystic female and probably antici-
pates that many students would seek her out for an everlasting life. Therefore, he explains the true meaning of immortality, telling us that not living
for oneself will lead us to "an everlasting life." He points to the most con-
spicuous example: Heaven and Earth. Then he invites us to ponder these
oxymora: sages remain behind yet lead; they ignore their own safety yet
endure; they are selfless yet self-realized. The deep principle behind these
seemingly contradictory phenomena is explained in chapter 23. Lao Tzu
probably thinks that students need to become familiar with the general
attributes of *Tao* before learning such an astounding principle.

8

上善若水。水善利萬物，而又爭居眾人之所惡，故幾於道。居善地，心善淵，與善天，言善信，政善治，事善能，動善時。夫唯不爭，故無尤。

> Great good is like water.
> Water is good at nourishing all things.
> It also[17] strives to settle in places people detest.
> So it is close to *Tao*.
> Goodness is to dwell lowly on the Earth;
>> still the mind in the deep of an abyss;
>> give freely after the way of Heaven;
>> speak sincerely;
>> govern justly;
>> work efficiently;
>> act in a timely way.
> Not striving with others procures no reproach.

COMMENTS

If sages do not exist for themselves, how do they live? Lao Tzu does not mention *how* directly; rather, he shows the goodness of water in seven areas that characterizes an entity not existing for itself. Hence, we shall know what to model ourselves after.

Lao Tzu begins by praising the nourishing virtue of water, commenting that "it also strives to settle..." He ends by praising the virtue of water for "not striving with others ..." Is he contradicting himself? Perhaps this is why the WB edition changes the word "also" to the word "not" (see note below).

---

17   This word *also* (*you* 又) is in the MWD text. The WB edition uses the word *not* (*bu* 不) instead: "It does not strive. It settles in places people detest."

When he comments in the beginning that water "strives to settle in places people detest," he effectively indicates water's virtue in not striving with anyone, because wherever it settles there will be no one with whom to strive. Is it because of this particular *striving* inclination that water is only *close* to *Tao* and not yet *Tao*?

Now let us examine how the sage models after water in its seven areas of goodness. Whenever water settles in a pond or lake, it is always in the lowest part of the landscape. This shows the virtue of humility. The sage stays lowly under all circumstances.

When water rests in the deep of an abyss, no wind can rouse any ripples. Thus, the sage stills the mind like water in an abyss; no temptation can stir it.

Water falls as rain from Heaven, acquiring no retribution. The sage benefits others without exacting retributions.

Whether water is murmuring in a small brook or roaring in a great river, its sound reflects the environment. Similarly the sage always speaks sincerely.

Water provides nourishment for all creatures without preference. Thus the sage is just and fair.

When water encounters small objects, it carries them along. When it encounters a large obstacle, it simply flows around it to continue its journey. This inspires the sage to manage affairs efficiently by incorporating workable suggestions while avoiding stubborn opposition.

Tides come and go punctually. The sage establishes good working habits and attends to matters in a timely fashion.

Lao Tzu says that water, with such high virtue in seven areas and humbly avoiding strife with everyone, is only close to *Tao*. Can we imagine how highly virtuous *Tao* is? Nay, *Tao* is beyond virtue, it is mystic virtue.

9

持而盈之，不如其已。揣而銳之，不可長保。金玉滿堂，莫之能守。富貴而驕，
自遺其咎。功遂身退，天之道也。

Fill the cup to the brim;
It is not so good as stopping in time.
Hone the blade edge overly sharp;
 the sharpness cannot be kept for long.
Amass a house full of gold and jade;
 no one can keep them secure.
Being wealthy and insolent,
 you leave only a legacy of calamities.
Retire when the work is done,
 this is the way of Heaven.

COMMENTS

If we aspire to be at one with *Tao*, we need more than to be like water.
Does this mean we have to try extra hard to the utmost of our ability?
Lao Tzu tells us not to go to extremes. The message in this verse is easy to
understand, but it may be hard to practice.

10

載營魄抱一，能無離乎？專氣致柔，能如嬰兒乎？滌除玄覽，能無疵乎？愛民
治國，能無智乎？天門開闔，能為雌乎？明白四達，能無知乎？生之、畜之，生
而弗有，長而弗宰。是為玄德。

> In keeping the soul and spirit as one,
> > can you prevent separation?
> In tuning the vital energy to softness,
> > can you become as an infant?
> In cleansing inner vision,
> > can you keep it free of blur?
> In loving people and governing the nation,
> > can you avoid cleverness?
> In opening and shutting the gate of Heaven,
> > can you act like a female?[18]
> When enlightened and seeing every corner,
> > can you remain innocent?
> Produce and nurture;
> > produce without possessiveness;[19]
> > rear without control.
> This is the mystic virtue.

COMMENTS

In chapter 8, Lao Tzu exhorts us to emulate water in our dealings with the
world. Here, he focuses on our inner development to attain mystic virtue.
Taoist initiates, with the guidance of a teacher, may read this chapter with

---

18   Taoists hold that the gate of Heaven is open and shut at the same time. It opens for
    inner vision and shuts out the physical senses. At that moment it is most advantage
    that the practitioner acts like a female: still, humble, and receptive.

19   This line and the next are variants of lines in chapter 2, "They let all things arise
    freely. They produce without possessiveness."

deeper insight. We can glean only its general philosophy and supplement that with teachings from Anthroposophy. It teaches that the human being consists of four members: the "I," an astral body, an etheric body, and a physical body (see appendix 1). Each has its function and intricately influences and assists the others. We venture to say that Lao Tzu informs us about how to harmonize these four members.

According to Anthroposophy, the "I" (or self) consists of two parts. The lower part is the soul, and the higher part is the spirit, or the Christ—that is, the Christ as in the teachings of St. Paul: "Not I, but the Christ in me."[20] Taoists refer yo the lower self as "the guest" and the higher self as "the host," or "the real-being" (zhen-ren 真人), the Tao in disguise.[21] The mind is part of the soul, and the spirit guides the mind through the will. When we flood the mind with desires, we can barely recognize the existence of the spirit, let alone follow its guidance. Thus the very first step for a Taoist student is to practice calming and stilling the mind so that soul (the guest) and spirit (the host) can coordinate harmoniously as one.

Anthroposophy explains that the astral body is the instrument for our feelings and perceptions. It should cooperate with but not dominate the mind (soul). However, many people are easily affected by their feelings and consequently their thinking becomes erratic. Taoists observe that heavy breathing signifies erratic thoughts. When the mind is calm, breathing softens. So Lao Tzu teaches students to train their breathing to become as soft and supple as that of an infant. When the breath is supple like that of a newborn, the mind will become innocent as a newborn as well. Recall in chapter 3, he suggests, "Empty the mind." Here, he shows that softening the breath is a means to emptying the mind.

---

20 See Sit, *The Lord's Prayer*, p. 57.

21 Ibid., pp. 15.

The etheric body records all our life experiences. Once we have cleansed our mind, we can have a clear view of our life record like that of a great tableau (also called a life review), access to the spiritual realm, and appreciate our relationship to the cosmos. Those who have a near-death experience frequently report a life review as part of their experience in the spiritual world. At death, we have this life review automatically (see appendix 1). Anthroposophy teaches exercises that can enable us to view the life tableau before death and access the spiritual realm and know the host. Here Lao Tzu does not elaborate on this inner vision. In chapter 16, he talks about the inner vision again in general terms (with no mention of the life tableau).

The function of the physical body is to carry out our will through action. When our action is infused with clarity of the spirit and without artful cleverness of the intellect, then we naturally become a role model without egoism.

When we have the four bodily members functioning harmoniously, we become naturally humble and quiet like a female, open to the inner guidance of *Tao,* and disregard outer sensual lures. Henceforth we invoke the practice of the mystic virtue: "produce and nurture; produce without possessiveness; rear without control."

11

三十輻共一轂，當其無，有車之用。埏埴以為器，當其無，有器之用。鑿戶牖以
為室，當其無，有室之用。故有之以為利，無之以為用。

> Thirty spokes share one hub.
> It is the empty center that enables the wheel to function.
> Knead clay into a vessel.
> It is the empty space that renders the vessel useful.
> Cut out doors and windows for a room.
> It is these empty spaces that make the room livable.
> Therefore the tangible (*you*) is for convenience.
> The intangible (*wu*) is for use.

COMMENTS

Recall that in chapter 1 we tried to use the wave–particle duality of a photon to illustrate the concurrent existence of *you* and *wu*. Here, Lao Tzu
provides three simple examples.

We may comprehend the coexistence of *you* and *wu*, yet it is still easy
to overlook the intangible *wu* aspect of objects and become enamored
with the tangible *you*. We need to remind ourselves constantly that the
pursuit of the material *you* hinders our progress in *Tao*.

12

五色令人目盲；五音令人耳聾；五味令人口爽；馳騁畋獵，令人心發狂；難得之貨，令人行妨。是以聖人為腹不為目，故去彼取此。

> The five colors dazzle human eyes.
> The five tones deafen our ears.
> The five flavors ruin the palate.
> Chasing and hunting wildly excites one's mind.
> "Hard-to-get goods" hinder our progress.
> Therefore, sages attend to the belly but not the eyes.[22]
> Therefore, they disregard the without
> and take care of the within.[23]

COMMENTS

In chapter 11 we learn that the tangible *you* of things is only for our convenience. It is better to view the tangible as a straw dog, without sentiment (chapter 5). When we are deluded by tangible colors, sounds, and flavors, our mind will be as one chasing about wildly while hunting. Our progress toward *Tao* will be hindered by our desire for hard-to-get goods. "Therefore, sages attend to the belly but not the eyes." Only by rejecting outer distractions can we empty the mind to know our true self. So the sage always disregards the without and takes care of the within.

---

22   Cf. chapter 3: "Empty the mind and fill the belly."

23   Literally, "Therefore, they reject that and take this."

13

寵辱若驚，貴大患若身。何謂寵辱若驚？寵之為下，得之若驚，失之若驚，是謂
寵辱若驚。何謂貴大患若身？吾所以有大患者，為吾有身也，及吾無身，有何
患？故貴為身於為天下，若可以托天下矣；愛以身為天下，如何以寄天下？

> Favor, like disgrace, is alarming.
> Treasure calamities as you do your body.
> What is the meaning of "Favor, like disgrace, is alarming"?
> Favor is inferior:
>> gain it and you are alarmed,
>> lose it and you are alarmed.
> That is the meaning of "Favor, like disgrace, is alarming."
> What is the meaning of "Treasure calamities as you do your body"?
> We have calamity because we have a body.
> If we did not have a body, what calamities could we have?
> Hence, if we value the body more than the empire,
>> we can be the custodians of the empire.
> If we like to use the body for the empire,
>> how can we be entrusted with the empire? [24]

COMMENTS

When we become detached from materialistic desires, we can view the
nature of so-called good fortune and misfortune in a very different way.

---

24 This whole chapter is from the MWD text. It is more streamlined than the one
in the WB edition. Both Text A and Text B of the MWD are essentially the same
(with almost no missing words) except the very last line, which differs in just one
word, with *how* [*can*] (*he* 何) in Text A, versus *can* (*ke* 可) in Text B. Using the
word *how* [*can*], we render the clause (如何以寄天下) as an inquiry: "how can we
be entrusted with the empire?" On the contrary, using the word *can* we read the
clause (如可以寄天下) affirmatively: "we can be entrusted with the empire." Thus,
in Text A, the clause conveys a doubt; but in Text B (as in the WB edition), it
expresses assurance. We deem that Text A (which was scripted earlier than Text
B) better integrates the overall message of this chapter. Please see the comments
on this chapter for further discussion.

Lao Tzu uses an oxymoron to shock us into examining the ways that good and bad fortunes may affect us.

Superficially, favor seems to be good fortune and desirable. Yet, if we ponder the way it may fetter us, we discover that favor is not really a boon. When someone bestows a favor upon us, we may wonder why we have received it. What obligations do we have? Will we soon lose it? When we lose a favor (no one can keep a favor forever), we may be greatly distressed by the ensuing disgrace. Therefore, favor is not really something to desire.

In general, people utterly dislike calamities. Yet, calamity is really a blessing in disguise. Those who experience a calamity such as a life-threatening illness invariably express gratitude after their recovery: "My illness (cancer, heart attack, stroke, and so on) was the best thing that ever happened to me. It gave me a chance to examine my priorities, helped me discover my true calling, and led me to live a more fulfilling life." As long as we have a body, we are certain to live through calamities. So we may as well treasure calamities as we do our body.

Lao Tzu invites us to look far and deeply into events and to resist becoming confused by their superficial glamor or discomfort. Through soul-searching efforts, we gain penetrating insights into so-called good and bad fortunes.

It is enlightening to learn that the attitude of rulers toward the body greatly influences how they rule. Lao Tzu tells us that one who values the body more than the empire can be a blessing to the empire, and that one who likes to use the body for the empire can ruin the empire. His comment seems paradoxical. Yet, if we examine rulers through history, we will appreciate his insight.

Let us take a closer look at those who like to use the body for the empire. Lao Tzu probably sees such individuals as ambitious, not hesitating to use their own body, and by extension the bodies of their subordinates, for gain (wealth and power) through the empire. When such persons are in power, they bring great suffering to their countries. A few notable examples in history—such as the First Emperor of Qin 秦始皇 in ancient China, Mao Tze-Tung 毛澤東 in modern China, and Adolf Hitler in Nazi Germany—support Lao Tzu's assertion.

Let us now study those who value the body more than the empire. Such a person respects life more than material wealth. When such individuals are in power, the people can live peacefully. These rulers may be rare and less familiar to us. Let us quote two examples from *Chuang Tzu*. The first is a great king called Dan-Fu 亶父, the grandfather of King Wen 文王 (1099–1050 B.C.E.) of the Zhou dynasty:

> Dan-Fu and his people originally lived in a place called Bin 邠. A barbarian tribe named Di 狄 repeatedly attacked Bin and rejected all of Dan-Fu's tribute of treasures. Finally Dan-Fu, who did not want war with the Di tribe, informed his people that he decided to cede Bin to the Di elders, moving himself to an undeveloped place called Qi-Shan 岐山. Upon his departure, his people willingly moved with him. Hence, he was able to establish a new nation at Qi-Shan.[25]

Dan-Fu had rather lost his wealth and power than the life of people in war. Thus his people knew he can be their custodian. They did not want to stay behind to be governed by the Di elders who used the body for power and wealth.

The second example is a marquis called Han Zhao Hou 韓昭侯 (r. 362–333 B.C.E.). He, indubitably, treasured his two arms.

> The two states Han 韓 and Wei 魏 were disputing over a parcel of conquered land. A Wei minister went to Han to negotiate with its marquis, Han Zhao Hou. He presented the marquis with a hypothetical

---

25 *Chuang Tzu*, chapter 28 (paraphrased). See, for example, Palmer and Breuilly, *The Book of Chuang Tzu*, p. 250.

proposition. "Suppose there were a treaty with these words, 'The arm that grabs this treaty will become disabled. Yet the one who gets the treaty will become the lord of the empire.'" He then asked whether the marquis would grab the treaty. Han Zhao Hou answered that he would not. The minister then commented, "You must consider your two arms to be more valuable than the empire. Now the body is much more precious than two arms, and a parcel of land is worth much less than the empire. Why do we wage war over this land by losing many precious bodies?" Han Zhao Hou was greatly impressed by the wisdom of this Wei minister.[26]

These examples confirm Lao Tzu's acute insight into human nature. May we have the wisdom needed to choose rulers who value the body more than the empire.

---

26 Ibid. (paraphrased); see also Plamer, p. 251.

14

視之不見，名曰微；聽之不聞，名曰希；搏之不得，名曰夷。此三者，不可致詰，故混而為一。一者，其上不皦，其下不昧，繩繩兮不可名，復歸於無物。是謂無狀之狀，無物之象，是謂惚恍。迎之不見其首，隨之不見其后。執今之道，以御今之有，以知古始，是謂道紀。

Look at it, but see it not; we call it the "invisible."
Listen to it, but hear it not; we call it the "inaudible."
Stroke it, but feel it not; we call it the "intangible."
These three are unfathomable, so we blend them as one.
This one,
> above it is not bright;
> below it is not dark.
Threading on continually, it is indefinable
> and returns beyond the realm of things.[27]
It is the form of the formless, the image of no thing.
It is fuzzy and hazy.
Meeting it you do not see its head.
Following it you do not see its back.
Embrace this *Tao* of the present:[28]
You can direct matters of the present,
> and you can know the origin of antiquity.
This is the doctrine of *Tao*.

---

27 Cf. chapter 6: "Lingering like a thread, she barely seems to exist."

28 The WB edition uses the word *ancient* (*gu* 古); hence, the line reads, "Embrace this Tao of the ancient" (執古之道). However, we like the word *present* (*jin* 今), used by the MWD text. *Present* evokes the idea that *Tao* is eternal, transcending time and always in the present.

COMMENTS

In chapter 11, Lao Tzu explains how to perceive the togetherness of *you* and *wu* in objects. Then, in chapter 13, he talks about how events do not appear as they seem to be. Favor may not be a boon, and calamity can be a blessing. We cannot fix a rule to nail down *Tao*. Here, he explores further the ethereal aspects of *Tao*. It is invisible, inaudible, and intangible, yet it exists as the valley spirit does. It may be fuzzy and hazy to many of us. However, if we follow the doctrine of *Tao,* we can manage the affairs of the present and know the origin of antiquity.

We may be puzzled over how embracing *Tao* can discern the origin of antiquity. The teachings of Anthroposophy show that it is possible to know the past if we have developed our spiritual "organs" and are able to read the akashic (or etheric) record. The recent discovery of a Lao Tzu document, "The Great One Excretes Water" (*Taiyi Shengshui* 太一生水, see appendix 2), also attests to this possibility. In chapter 16, Lao Tzu tells us how to observe life returning to its origin.

15

古之善為道者，微妙玄達，深不可識。夫唯不可識，故強為之容：豫兮，若冬涉川；猶兮，若畏四鄰；儼兮，其若客；渙兮，其若凌釋；敦兮，其若樸；曠兮，其若谷；混兮，其若濁。濁以靜之徐清。安以動之徐生。保此道者，不欲盈。夫唯不欲盈，故能蔽而不成。

Taoist adepts of old were profound, subtle, mystical, and insightful.
They are too deep to be known.
Because they are abstruse,
    we can describe only how they appear:
Hesitant, as when fording a stream in winter;
    cautious, as in fear of one's surrounding neighbors;
    respectful, like a guest;
    yielding like ice starting to melt;
    simple as uncut wood;
    open like a valley;
    opaque as a puddle.
By being still, they can change from murkiness to clarity.
By activity, they can change from quietude to animation.
Those who treasure this *Tao* do not want to be full.
Not wanting to be full, they can remain hidden and incomplete.

COMMENTS

If *Tao* is fuzzy, hazy, and unfathomable, as stated in chapter 14, then it is no easier to learn about its adept practitioners. In fact—*as above, so below*—the characteristics of a Taoist master are not much different from those of *Tao*. Yet, with great ingenuity, Lao Tzu is able to delineate the essence of such masters vividly. He mentions that his description is about Taoist masters of old. Thus he hints that, during his own time, this kind of master has become very rare and virtually nonexistent. We can imagine that Lao Tzu was one among the existing few.

In chapter 8, Lao Tzu uses one element—water—to demonstrate seven attributes of *Tao*. Here, he employs seven simple images to illustrate the traits of Taoist masters. These are essentially the characteristics of a humble person. The image of uncut wood for simplicity is a favorite of Lao Tzu, and he uses it again in chapters 19, 28, 32, 37, and 57.

Humble individuals do not want to be full for two particular reasons. First, they want to avoid drawing attention. Consequently, they become seclusive. Second, they never consider themselves perfect; they always look for room to improve, as if they were incomplete.

16

致虛，極也。守靜，篤也。萬物并作，吾以觀其復也。夫物芸芸，各復歸其根。
歸根曰靜，靜是謂復命。復命常也，知常明也。不知常妄，妄作，凶。知常容，
容乃公，公乃王，王乃天，天乃道，道乃殁身不殆。

> Attain emptiness to the far end.
> Keep stillness in the deep bottom.
> All things arise together.
> We thereby observe their return.
> All things grow and flourish,
>   yet each one returns to its root.
> To return to the root is to keep stillness.
> Keeping stillness means recovering life.
> Recovering life is the norm.[29]
> Knowing the norm, one is illumined.
> Not knowing the norm,
>   one is confused and may act erratically.
> That is disastrous.
> Knowing the norm, one is embracing.
> Being embracing, one is impartial.
> Being impartial, one is kingly.
> Being kingly, one is heavenly.
> Being heavenly, one is at one with *Tao*.
> Being at one with *Tao*,
>   one suffers no harm to the end of life.

COMMENTS

Some Taoists hold that this chapter provides the key to longevity. It is
about how to go back to the "root," the source of life. In chapter 6, Lao

---

29 The norm is the way of nature.

Tzu says that the valley spirit never dies and is the gateway to the root of Heaven and Earth. Thus returning to the root by stilling one's mind can be a means transcending the cycle of birth and death and prolonging life indefinitely. Other Taoist masters explain, however, that the idea of longevity is only an inducement to get people to practice stilling the mind. Most of the imagery in Taoism is aimed at spiritual advancement rather than at physical longevity.[30] The depth and insightfulness of ancient Taoist masters was possible because they diligently practiced stilling the mind and emptying desire.

The human mind is boundless in width and depth. The far end and the deep bottom are only figures of speech, signifying that the mind can roam far and deep. There is no limit on how much we can advance in this practice. As the mind empties, we become more open, receptive, and embracing. As the mind is stilled, we are less likely to become aroused by greed, loathing, and craving. The Western esoteric tradition embraces this practice, as well. In *How to Know Higher Worlds*, Steiner suggests, "Bring all the thoughts that habitually ebbed and flowed within you to rest. Become perfectly still and inwardly silent" (pp. 90–91).

After extensive practice, we can have clear inner vision and understand the revealing and non-revealing functions of *Tao*. We know then how all things arise together and how each disintegrates, returning to stillness. We understand the normal cycle of life: growing and decaying. Returning to our root is therefore our means to recovering life. We will not act erratically once we have this understanding of how life regenerates. Thus, we will hurt no one. Knowing that all things arise from the same source and have their own time and place for growth, we will not violate their rights and intrude into their spaces. We become compassionate and tolerant. We will act impartially, like a just king, becoming a role

---

30 See Sit, *The Lord's Prayer*, pp. 138–139.

model and leading others.[31] Whoever follows the way of Heaven is automatically at one with *Tao*. Such a person acts like water, "not striving with others" (chapter 8). Such a person accrues no reproach and suffers no harm to the end of life.

---

31 We will explore more fully what the "king" signifies in chapter 25.

17

太上，下知有之；其次，親譽之；其次，畏之；其下，侮之。信不足焉，有不信
焉。悠兮，其貴言。功成事遂，而百姓謂：「我自然」。

> The best leaders are barely noticed.
> The next are those fondly praised.
> The next are those feared.
> The worst are those despised.
> If you are not trustworthy, others will not trust you.
> Being taciturn, sages treasure their word.
> When their task is completed successfully,
> > they let the people say,
> > "It just happened to us naturally."

COMMENTS

We can alternately read the beginning four lines as commentary on the four
historical phases of leaders: "In antiquity, leaders are barely noticed. Next,
they are fondly praised. Next, they are feared. Lastly, they are despised."
This alternate reading which not only shows the four types of leaders as
interpreted above, is also more in tone with the discourse in chapters 18
and 19.

In chapter 16, Lao Tzu states that those who cultivate stillness have the
potential to be leaders. When they become leaders, they will be the best
kind of leaders. Their maxim will be, "When work is done, retiring is the
way of Heaven" (chapter 9). Hence, they naturally draw no attention to
themselves.

The worst leaders are those who serve only their own ambitions and
rule by controlling people. When one set of rules fails to work, such leaders create another set to override the previous set. Thereby, they lose the

people's trust. By contrast, the best leaders care only for the people. Without ado, they nurture people to be innocent without cleverness and non-discriminative without desires (chapter 3). The best leaders understand that rules and laws always create loopholes through which people may sneak. The least amount of legislation leads people to attend to their own business naturally. However, according to the alternate reading, the best kind of political rulers were virtually nonexistent in Lao Tzu's time.

18

故大道廢，有仁義；智慧出，有大偽；六親不和，有孝慈；邦家昏亂，有貞臣。

> Therefore, when the Great *Tao* recedes,
>   humanity and morality emerge.
> When knowledge and cleverness appear,
>   great artificiality begins.
> When the six relations[32] are in discord,
>   people appreciate filial piety and parental kindness.
> When the nation is benighted and chaotic,
>   loyal ministers stand out.

COMMENTS

"The best leaders are barely noticed" (chapter 17). In an orderly society, most people rarely notice the loyal ministers. However, when a nation is in turmoil, people will realize their importance. Similarly, when a family is in harmony, its members seldom appreciate the caring parents and the devoting offspring. When a family is in discord, however, its members recognize their significance. Therefore, it is natural that the withdrawal of the great *Tao* brings out an acute yearning in people for benevolence and justice. Such a yearning moves many to resort to the intellect, creating a great deal of artifice.

When the Great *Tao* recedes, people can no longer detect its outward guidance as easily. Yet, *Tao* does not abandon us. It is now within us as the little voice of our conscience, or, in Taoist terms, *Tao* is hidden as the

---

32 The six relations are: parents and offspring, elder and younger siblings, husbands and wives.

"real being."[33] We gradually are to develop the intellectual mind to decide freely how to heed the call of our conscience.

As stated in the preface (p. viii) and detailed in appendix 1, human consciousness evolves over long eons. We begin with a dim, trance-like consciousness and gradually develop to a clear, wakeful, sentient consciousness. Before (and even during) our development of the sentient consciousness, people had a kind of dreamy consciousness and a vague awareness of guidance from the spiritual world. They could perceive messages of the "gods" through oracles or through divination of special signs in nature. However, if we continue to receive such outward guidance, we will never evolve to become free beings. This situation is analogous to raising a child. In order to help their children become independent adults, parents gradually recede into the background as children reach a certain age. When human beings are ready to become independent, the great *Tao* slowly recedes into the background. It is still present, but we pay little or no attention to it. While we remain keenly focused on material sustenance and trust only our sensory perceptions, we ignore subtle spiritual signals.

Anthroposophy teaches that the withdrawal of the spiritual world (*Tao*) is gradual. During the long weaning process, guidance is provided latently. There are mystery centers where advanced masters teach students how to understand hidden messages of the spiritual world. Once the initiates complete their training, they may assist the rulers directly or simply live among the common people as role models. Chapter 15 shows what those ancient initiates are like, and chapters 10 and 16 provide a glimpse of their training. Chapter 17 may be read as a chronicle of how rulers can gradually deteriorate from the best to the worst as *Tao* recedes.

Henceforth, when people practice the suggestions in chapters 10 and 16, they can discern the way of *Tao* from within. Nevertheless, even if

---

33 See comments in chapter 10.

direct, outward guidance of *Tao* is no longer prominent and the inner vision of *Tao* has yet to develop, there are still discernible working principles of *Tao* in the world. When we observe and follow them, we can enrich our lives significantly. In the *Tao Te Ching*, Lao Tzu shows how to weave these clearly observable principles into our daily living.

19

絕聖棄智，民利百倍；絕仁棄義，民復孝慈；絕巧棄利，盜賊無有。此三言也以
為文，不足。故令有所屬：見素抱樸，少私寡欲。

> Banish sagacity, discard cleverness,
>> and the people will benefit a hundredfold.
>
> Banish humanity, discard righteousness,
>> and the people will again be filial and kind.
>
> Banish craftiness, discard profiteering,
>> and thieves and robbers will disappear.
>
> These three sayings are formal outlines and are insufficient.
>
> Indeed, one needs to follow a different ideal:
>> observe purity and embrace simplicity;[34]
>
>> diminish selfishness and minimize cravings.

COMMENTS

During the period when Lao Tzu lived, the central authority of the emperor
had declined, leaving many regional states to contend for domination of
the empire. Wars and conflicts became the norm. Many "men of knowledge" considered themselves political experts and traveled the states to
peddle their strategies. Some suggested rites and rules to keep order; others promoted severe punishments to eliminate the unruly. To Lao Tzu,
humanity and justice are artifices that maintain social harmony only tem-
porarily. Understanding human nature, he could see such strategies do not
work in the long run.[35]

Seeing through cause and effect, Lao Tzu makes three formal suggestions. He reiterates, however, that to eradicate the true cause of social
unrest, people must "diminish selfishness and minimize cravings."

---

34 Literally this line reads: Appear like raw silk and embrace uncut wood.

35 See chapters 57–58, and 65.

20

絕學無憂。唯之與訶,相去幾何?美之與惡,其相去何?若人之所畏,亦不可以不畏?恍兮,其未央哉!眾人熙熙,如享太牢,如春登台。我獨泊兮,其未兆,如嬰兒之未咳;儽儽兮,若無所歸。眾人皆有餘,而我獨若遺。我愚人之心也哉,沌沌兮!俗人昭昭,我獨昏昏。俗人察察,我獨悶悶。忽兮,其若海。恍兮,若無所止。眾人皆有以,而我獨頑似鄙。吾欲獨異於人,而貴食母。

Drop learning and you will no longer worry.
Respectful response and loud scold,
    how much do they differ?
Beauty and ugliness,
    how wide is the difference?
As to what others hold in awe,
    should you not do so as well? [36]
Too foggy; see no end to it!
Most people like parties and festivities.
They feast on the ox after the great sacrifice;
    they climb terraces to sightsee in spring.
I alone am unperturbed, revealing no sign,
    like a newborn who has not yet smiled.
Desolate, as if having no home to which I return.
Most people have extra.
I alone seem to be left out.
I have the mind of a fool, completely turbid.
Others are so bright; I alone am dim.
Others are so keen; I alone am dull.
Pending, I roll like the sea.

---

36   This clause is from the WB. In the MWD, there is an extra word people (*ren* 人) at the end, 亦不可以不畏人. Hence, the line is read as, "As to those whom others respect, should you not respect them as well?" However, Lao Tzu then illustrates that most people like sight-seeing, gaining wealth, and so on, with no mention of "respecting others." In this regard, the WB is more coherent.

Unsettling, I find nowhere to stop.
Most people have ambitions and means;
   I alone am stubborn and scanty.
My goal is different from others,
   for I value being nourished by the mother.

COMMENTS

In chapter 19, Lao Tzu recommends diminishing selfishness and minimizing cravings to rediscover the guidance of *Tao* from within. In this chapter, he describes vividly how such Taoist practitioners live.

Since Taoists attend to the inner and not to the outer; they are not perturbed by the hustle and bustle of society. They do not spend time learning artificial social constructs. They do not worry about how others judge their behavior. They do not confuse the essential with the superficial. To dramatize how such a Taoist differs from others, Lao Tzu poses several questions about matters that most people deem important, but to which a Taoist will pay no heed.

Whereas others actively pursue material enjoyment, Taoists, like fools, neglect such pursuits. They are not alert and bright like others, because they have no interest in things of the world. They follow only the inner guidance of *Tao*. However, *Tao* is hidden so deeply that Taoists cannot be sure that they will always understand the prompts. Thus, Taoists seem like they have no home in which to settle and lack something. They are always "hesitant, as when fording a stream in winter" (chapter 15). Yet they diligently follow this advice: "Observe purity and embrace simplicity. Diminish selfishness and minimize cravings" (chapter 19). They do not let the five colors, tones, and tastes hinder their progress toward *Tao* (chapter 12). They are innocent like an infant and value only the mother's nourishment.

21

孔德之容，惟道是從。道之為物，惟恍惟惚。惚兮恍兮，其中有象；恍兮惚兮，
其中有物；窈兮冥兮，其中有精；其精甚真，其中有信。自今及古，其名不去，
以順眾甫。吾何以知眾甫之然也？以此。

> The greatest virtue is solely to follow *Tao*.
> *Tao* as a thing is actually fuzzy and hazy;
>> hazy and fuzzy, yet it has an image;
>> fuzzy and hazy, yet it has substance;
>> dark and dim, yet it has an essence.
> This essence is very real and can be trusted.
> From the present, going back to antiquity,
>> its Name has never gone away.
> It harmonizes the fathers[37] of the multitude.
> How do I know the multitude fathers are so?
> It is by this.[38]

COMMENTS

This chapter serves as a brief summary of the beginning chapters. Here, Lao Tzu delineates *Tao* in a slightly different shade while reflecting most of the themes in chapters 1, 4, 6, 14 and 15. He adds that, when one understands the significance of this ancient Name *"Tao,"* one can flow harmoniously with all things.

Let us reiterate one important point in our study. In antiquity, human beings had various ways of learning the guidance of *Tao*. During the early stage of human evolution, people had dreamlike consciousness of *Tao* (see comments in chapter 18). This dreamlike consciousness is probably the reason that Lao Tzu repeatedly mentions the fuzziness and haziness of

---

37 *Father* means the origin. Each thing has its own origin.

38 It is by knowing what the Name signifies.

Tao. People gradually developed sentient consciousness to comprehend the physical world clearly while losing direct contact with *Tao*. Nevertheless, *Tao* never disappears. *Tao* is difficult to perceive from the outside when we are distracted by a myriad of sensual activities. Henceforth, the way to *Tao* is mainly from within. *Tao* is hidden deep within, and we can discern it only when our mind is still.

In the next three chapters,[39] Lao Tzu reveals the principle of bestowing, a simple yet astounding virtue of *Tao*.

---

39 Those three chapters are entirely from the MWD text. We think that the WB edition has altered them too much for a coherent reading. Please note that chapter 24 comes before chapters 22 and 23.

24

吹者不立。自視者不彰；自見者不明；自伐者無功；自矜者不長。其在道也，曰
餘食贅形，物或惡之，故有欲者弗居。

> Those who blow cannot establish their virtues.
> Those who justify themselves are not manifest;
>> those who flaunt themselves are not illustrious;
>> those who boast of themselves gain no merit;
>> those who brag about themselves cannot endure.
> From the standpoint of *Tao*,
>> they are like leftover food and tumor growths.
> Even creatures seem to detest them;
>> thus, people who have desires avoid them.

COMMENTS

This chapter is essentially about arrogant people who go on about themselves. Lao Tzu reiterates this theme in grades: justifying, flaunting, boasting, and bragging. Sages are so humble that they never engage in such talk. Those who behave this way are people who desire to be manifest, to be illustrious, to gain merit, and to endure. Yet their actions do not help them achieve their desires. Shouldn't they avoid such actions?

22

曲則全，枉則正，窪則盈，敝則新，少則得，多則惑。是以聖人抱一為天下牧。
不自視，故彰；不自見，故明；不自伐，故有功；不自矜，故能長。夫唯不爭，故
天下莫能與之爭。古之所謂「曲則全」者，豈虛言哉！誠全而歸之。

Wrong can become whole.
The crooked can be straightened.
Hollow can be filled.
The worn can be renewed.
When you have little you may gain.
When you have much you may be deluded.
So sages embrace unity
    and become shepherds of the world.
Not justifying themselves, thus they are manifest;
Not flaunting themselves, thus they are illustrious;
Not boasting of themselves, thus they gain merit;
Not bragging about themselves, thus they endure.
By not contending,
    no one in the world can contend with them.
Indeed, ancient sayings[40] such as
    "Wrong can become whole" are not empty talk.
Truly, they all guide back to unity.

COMMENTS

Before continuing the theme in chapter 24, Lao Tzu reminds us with six
ancient sayings on the nature of polarities (cf. chapter 2). When one does
wrong, one has an opportunity to become whole. After one attains whole-
ness, it may be temporary. Many occasions still exist to do wrong again.
Similarly, when one has little, one may gain; but when one gains too much,

---

40   The ancient sayings refer to the beginning six lines.

one may be deluded and begin to lose. Sages understand this principle very well and do not hold onto either pole; thus they embrace unity and transcend duality. By doing so, they become "shepherds" of the world. A shepherd is one who embraces the entire flock, leaving no one out. We shall comment further on this attribute of a shepherd in chapter 27.

Sages who are naturally humble do not show off. They do not justify themselves, flaunt themselves, boast, or brag. However, behaving by avoiding blowing enables them to be manifest, to be illustrious, to gain merit, and to endure. Furthermore, they never contend with anyone. If they contend, they must cling to something to hold against others. They are well aware that whatever they hold onto is not going to stay with them forever. Everything oscillates, just as the moon waxes and wanes. So they contend with no one and cling to nothing except following unity.

Now let us compare the assertions in chapter 24 and in this one. In chapter 24, Lao Tzu observes that there are certain behaviors that do not bring the desired results. To achieve the desired results, people should avoid those behaviors as they would spoiled leftover food. Here, in this chapter, he points out that sages—those of *Tao* and not those with desires—naturally avoid behaving in that way. Yet, by not behaving that way, they attain the results that people who behave that way have missed. Is this not baffling?

23

希言自然。飄風不終朝，暴雨不終日。孰為此？天地。天地尚不能久，而況於人乎？故從事於道者同於道。德者同於德；失者同於失。同於德者，道亦德之；同於失者，道亦失之。

> To speak little is the way of nature.
> Gusty winds don't last all morning.
> Torrential rains don't last all day.
> What makes them so?
> Heaven and Earth do.
> Even Heaven and Earth cannot sustain that long;
> > how much less can people.
> So those who practice the way of *Tao* are at one with *Tao*.
> Those who practice the way of gain are at one with gain.[41]
> Those who practice the way of loss are at one with loss.
> When they are at one with gain,
> > *Tao* gains with them.
> When they are at one with loss,
> > *Tao* loses with them.

COMMENTS

In this chapter, we learn the principle of the bestowing virtue of *Tao*. Whence we may no longer find the phenomena discussed in chapters 24 and 22 baffling.

According to Lao Tzu, the bestowing virtue of *Tao* works like a copy machine. It always reproduces what we have intended. Recall that, in chapter 4, he uses an empty vessel to hint that we always get what we wish

---

41 The word *te* 德 can be translated as at least these words: *gain, conduct, potency, success,* or *virtue*. We consider the meaning of *gain* to be more fitting in this context, since it contrasts with *loss* in the next line.

for. Next, in chapter 5, he illustrates that what we get is what we have in mind, as a bellows: "air in, air out." Last, in chapter 6, he reiterates this reflective attribute of *Tao* with an image of the valley that echoes our calls. From these examples, we see that *Tao* is not deciding what we may get. It functions only as a facilitator that helps us get what we have intended. We reap what we have sowed.

Now, knowing that *Tao* always facilitates what we have intended, we may ask: Why do we not always get what we desire? Is this because we have subtly shifted our intent without being aware? When people desire to gain something, they become impatient and hope to get it as quickly as possible. They cannot "act in a timely way" (chapter 8). When people do not get what they desire soon enough, they fret and pine for it. Thus, they unconsciously change their original desire to gain something into a desire to *want* to gain something. Their want reflects their worry about *losing* it. Hence, many, owing to their worry, unwittingly shift an intent of gaining to an intent of wanting, which in effect, is equivalent to an intent of losing.

Most people probably have some vague knowledge of this principle but cannot calm the mind and cease fretting. Thus, they repeatedly flip-flop and create a chaotic sequence of intentions. They sometimes gain, sometimes lose, and declare that it is because of their luck, or rather the lack of luck.

I comment on these aspects of gain and loss in my book *The Lord's Prayer* by using the phrase *persist–resist* to capture these apparent phenomena (p. 90). If we *persist* in gaining something, then that something will *resist* appearing for us. By contrast, if we *resist* having something, then that something will *persist* in appearing for us. Let us review chapters 24, 22, and 23 in terms of this *persist–resist* principle.

In chapter 24, the four examples directly illustrate the *persist–resist* principle. When we persist in gaining virtues such as manifestation by justifying ourselves and so on, then such virtues will resist appearing for us.

Next, in chapter 22, the four examples inversely shed light on the *persist–resist* principle. When we resist gaining virtues such as manifestation by not justifying ourselves and so on, then such virtues will persist in appearing for us. The oxymora in chapter 7—"sages remain behind yet can lead; they ignore their own safety yet can endure; they are selfless yet are self-realized"—are also the inverse examples of this principle.

Finally, in chapter 23, we learn the cause of this *persist–resist* principle: "When they are at one with gain, *Tao* gains with them. When they are at one with loss, *Tao* loses with them." It is a pity that so many people unknowingly practice the way of loss and are at one with loss.

Please take note that, whether we gain or lose, we do not gain or lose forever. Even Heaven and Earth cannot keep torrential rains or gusty winds for long. It is better to practice embracing unity without being sentimental about gain or loss. Therefore, sages practice only the way of *Tao* and become "at one with *Tao*."

25

有物混成，先天地生。寂兮寥兮，獨立而不改，周行而不殆，可以為天地母。
吾未知其名，字之曰道，強為之名曰大。大曰逝，逝曰遠，遠曰反。道大，天
大，地大，王亦大。國中有四大，而王居其一焉。人法地，地法天，天法道，
道法自然。

> There is something undifferentiated yet complete.
> It exists even before Heaven and Earth.
> Silent and boundless,
>> standing alone and unchanging,[42]
>> continually circulating yet never tired,
>> it can be considered the mother of Heaven and Earth.[43]
> I do not yet know its name[44] and refer to it as "*Tao*."
> If it must be named, I shall call it "Great."
> Great as if it disappears,
>> disappears to a far away place;
>> from a far away place it returns.[45]
> *Tao* is great;
> Heaven is great;
> Earth is great;
> The king is also great.
> In the realm there are four greats,
>> and the king is one of them.

---

42 The aspect that *Tao* is concurrently revealing and non-revealing is unchanging.
    See comments in chapter 1.

43 For more on the Taoist view of the creative process, see chapter 42 and appendix 2.

44 Compare the story of Moses in the Burning Bush. He asked God's name and God
    replied with the words "I am the 'I Am'" (Exodus 3:13–14).

45 Picture how a point moves around a circle. It always comes back to where it starts.
    We may consider the location diametrically opposite to the staring point as a far-
    away place. Then, whatever moves around the circle from the starting point will
    go to a far-away place and return. For a geometric discussion of this view, see Sit,
    The Lord's Prayer, pp. 34–36.

> People follow the way of Earth,
>   Earth follows the way of Heaven,
>   Heaven follows the way of *Tao*,
>   *Tao* follows what is natural.

COMMENTS

After disclosing the subtle bestowing virtue of *Tao*, Lao Tzu reiterates its mystic nature, expanding what he says in chapters 1 and 21. Disregard what name we designate to *Tao*. Its way is always a model for all people, especially those who aspire to become "king." It is vital that they follow the way of *Tao*. Kings can be political rulers, the heads of organizations, or simply individuals taking care of themselves. Indeed, our being is acutely in want of a true king (see comments in chapters 10, 16, and 18).

The character of the word king (*wang* 王) can be viewed as a symbol that encompasses the ideal (or destiny) of a human being. Let us inspect its character from two different script styles to discover its implications.

First, consider this character in its contemporary "regular script" (*kaishu* 楷書) style, as in the figure on the right below. In this style, it consists of three evenly spaced horizontal bars, with a vertical stroke connecting the top and the bottom through the middle. Suppose we regard the top as Heaven, the bottom as Earth, the middle as a person, with the vertical representing that person's ideals and actions, connecting Heaven and Earth. Thus, the character symbolizes human beings who harmonize their existence between Heaven and Earth.

Next, let us look at this character in the antique "seal script" (*chuanshu* 篆書) style, as in the left figure.

In this style the middle bar is not exactly at the middle but placed slightly higher. The character looks like a cross between two horizontal bars. We may regard the cross as a person with his arms stretched out between Heaven (the top) and Earth (the bottom). In this style, the character symbolizes those bearing their cross in the world.

This second symbol encompasses deep esoteric knowledge about humankind. In many of his Anthroposophy lectures, Steiner states that in esotericism the cross is a symbol for a human being with outstretched arms, and that Jesus Christ is a fulfillment of this symbolic archetype. With this esoteric knowledge about human beings and kings, we may see why Jesus Christ is revered as the King of Kings.

Whether we adopt the esoteric or a more general viewpoint of what the word *king* means, we now understand why the king is one of the four greats in the world. Furthermore we also know why the *Tao Te Ching* is not simply an instruction manual for the royal lords and monarchs, as commonly thought. In fact, it is a book dedicated to teaching people to fulfill their destinies as the "king." Shall we say we are all kings in the making?

26

重為輕根，靜為躁君。是以君子終日行不離其輜重。雖有榮觀，燕處超然。奈
何萬乘之王，而以身輕於天下？輕則失本，躁則失君。

> Heaviness is the root of lightness,
>> stillness is the master of unrest.
> Therefore, when sovereigns[46] travel all day,
>> they never part with their baggage wagon.
> However magnificent the views are,
>> they remain calm and detached.
> How can kings of ten thousand chariots
>> take themselves lighter than the empire?[47]
> If they take themselves lightly,
>> they lose their foundation.
> If they are restless,
>> they lose their self-mastery.

COMMENTS

After having indicated that the king is one of the four greats, Lao Tzu concentrates on teaching the way of kingliness, which is actually the way of *Tao*. Even though he concerns himself mainly with the broader meaning of kingliness, he does not shy away from using the activities of traditional kings as metaphors for his teaching. Human culture may keep changing and evolving, but the teaching of *Tao* will never be outdated.

Lao Tzu contrasts heaviness and stillness with lightness and unrest. Common sense informs us that, while light objects are easily disturbed,

---

46 The term *jun-zi* 君子 can mean "sovereign," "monarch," or refer to a person of nobility or gentility. We consider "sovereign" the most appropriate in this context. See also chapter 31 and appendix 2 for the use of this term.

47 Han Zhao Hou 韓昭侯 considered that even his two arms are heavier (more important) than the empire. See comments in chapter 13.

heavy objects are stable and hard to move. A stilled mind is like a heavy object and a stirring mind a light one.

Lao Tzu is not the only teacher who expounds on the practice of stilling the mind. Many teachers of other cultural traditions also shed light on this practice. For example, Mencius (390–305 B.C.E.), a highly respected Confucian philosopher, once told his disciples that he had achieved "not stirring his mind" at age forty. Or consider Gautama Buddha. His enlightenment story depicts him sitting, unmoving, in deep meditation for seven days under the bodhi tree. Buddhists usually meditate in a crossed-leg pose as the Buddha did, because such a pose can anchor one's body firmly and facilitate stilling the mind.

When we are outwardly heavy, it is less convenient for us to move around. When a situation is inconvenient, we may be less inclined to act hastily. Creating inconvenient situations can be conducive to cultivating inner stillness. According to his disciples, the Tibetan Lama Chögyam Trungpa Rinpoche was an expert in creating inconvenient situations to cultivate stillness. It is reported that he would arrange his furniture in a slightly inconvenient fashion or wear very tight clothing underneath a suit to practice being still and centered.[48]

The picture of sovereigns not parting their heavy baggage wagon illustrates how they create inconvenience to cultivate stillness. Owing to their heaviness, they become secure and serene. No matter how impressive the scenery may be, they can not be lured away from their path (practice). The benefits of being heavy and still cannot be overemphasized. Because heaviness is a means toward stillness, Lao Tzu henceforth discusses only stillness.

---

48 Pema Chödrön, *The Wisdom of No Escape: And the Path of Loving-Kindness*, pp. 94–95.

27

善行者無轍跡。善言者無瑕讁。善數者不用籌策。善閉者無關楗而不可啟也。
善結者無繩約而不可解也。是以聖人恒善救人，而無棄人，物無棄財，是謂襲
明。故善人，善人之師。不善人，善人之資也。不貴其師，不愛其資，雖知乎
大迷。是謂妙要。

> One who is good at walking leaves no tracks.
> One who is good at speech makes no slips.
> One who is good at reckoning uses no chips.
> One who is good at shutting doors uses neither bolt nor lock,
>> lest what is shut cannot be opened.
> One who is good at tying things uses no ropes,
>> lest what is tied cannot be loosened.[49]
> Therefore, sages are always good at saving people
>> and never abandon anyone.
> With things they never waste any material.
> This is called enlightened.
> Therefore, a good person is a teacher of goodness.[50]
> Those who are not good are the material for goodness.
> Not to value one's teacher,
>> not to treasure one's material,
>>> though learned, one is really gone astray.
> What is said may be intriguing yet important.

---

49 Traditionally the couplet is read as, "One who is good at shutting doors uses nei-
    ther bolt nor lock, yet what is shut cannot be opened. One who is good at tying
    things uses no ropes, yet what is tied cannot be loosened" (underlines added).
    Please see comments for the reason why we differ.

50 This line is from the MWD text. The WB edition reads: "Therefore a good person
    is a teacher for the non-good" (故善人者，不善人之師). The MWD text connotes
    a broader meaning. The good man as a role model is showing all people (not just
    the non-good) the conduct of goodness.

COMMENTS

Those who are heavy and still do not act erratically (chapter 26); they are naturally good at what they do. They are humble and never brag (chapter 22). "They accomplish without claiming credit" (chapter 2). Thus, in their walk of life, sages leave no tracks of their accomplishments. They "speak sincerely" (chapter 8), so they never slip up. They are unconcerned with losses or gains. They are well aware that, "When they are at one with gain, *Tao* gains with them. When they are at one with loss, *Tao* loses with them" (chapter 23). They know that, even as they are gaining, they cannot gain forever. Therefore they practice only the way of *Tao* and become "at one with *Tao*." Hence, they need no counting chips to reckon transactions.

Sages, who understand well the consequences of shutting doors with locks or bolts, will not use such a means to close a door, lest others cannot get in. Sages, who know well the results of tying things with a rope, will not tie things up with it, lest others cannot use the material. We may consider "tying things up with a rope" as a metaphor for limiting or confining people's potential. Thus, teachers who encourage students to develop all their latent potential will not tie things up.

Our reading of these two lines contradicts the traditional reading for two reasons. First, we observe that the sentence structure of this couplet is different from that of the beginning three lines. This difference signifies a shift of emphasis. Second (and more important), if we follow the traditional reading, how can we deduce in the next two lines—that sages abandon no one when doors are tightly shut, preventing others from entering, and they waste nothing when all things are intricately tied, preventing others from using?

Therefore, sages will shut no door and tie up nothing. Indeed, "sages embrace unity and become shepherds of the world" (chapter 22). A shepherd embraces the entire flock—both the good and the bad. The parable of a shepherd in the Gospels (Matthew 18:12–14 and Luke 15:3–7) aptly sheds light on this attitude of the sage. In this parable, the shepherd has a hundred sheep, but one strays away. The shepherd keeps looking for it until it is found. Thus, both the sage and the shepherd are truly enlightened.

A good person is a role model, showing goodness. A person who is not good, however, is not to be shut out and neglected and is the material for goodness. Lao Tzu always emphasizes the subtlety of unity. It is important that we care not only for the good, but also for those who are not good.

28

知其雄，守其雌，為天下谿。為天下谿，恒德不離。恒德不離，復歸於嬰兒。
知其白，守其黑，為天下式。為天下式，恒德不忒。恒德不忒，復歸於無極。
知其榮，守其辱，為天下谷。為天下谷，恒德乃足。恒德乃足，復歸於樸。
樸散則為器，聖人用則為官長。夫大制無割。

> Know the male,
>> abide by the female,[51]
>> and become a stream of the world.
> Being a stream of the world,
>> you do not part from the eternal virtue.
> Not parting from the eternal virtue,
>> you revert to an infant.[52]
> Know the light,
>> abide by the shade,
>> and become a model of the world.
> Being a model of the world,
>> you move unerringly with eternal virtue.
> Moving unerringly with eternal virtue,
>> you revert to the infinite.
> Know the glory,
>> abide by the defiled,
>> and become a valley of the world,
> Being a valley of the world,
>> you are filled with the eternal virtue.

---

51 According to Anthroposophy (see Appendix I), while men have a male physical body but a female etheric (life) body, women conversely have a female physical body but a male etheric body. In view of this, it is definitely important that we should know the one gender and abide by the other for balance.

52 Cf. chapter 10, "Can you become like an infant?" and chapter 20, "Like a newborn that has not yet smiled . . . "

Being filled with the eternal virtue,
  you revert to uncut wood.
When uncut wood is broken up,
  it may become a vessel.
But when sages serve,
  they become the chiefs of all officials.
Therefore, great governing does no splitting.[53]

COMMENTS

This chapter continues to show how sages cultivate oneness by embracing both poles. They make sure that they understand and maintain both the *yang* (the male, the light, and the honorable) and the *yin* (the female, the shade, and the lowly). The ideal of sages is to "embrace unity and become a shepherd of the world" (chapter 22).

Sages are like a stream, allowing all water from the mountain to converge without discrimination, like a pattern of light and shade harmoniously commingling, and like a valley open and receptive to all. Sages naturally return to the innocence of an infant, the inexhaustibility of the infinite, and the simplicity of uncut wood.

A vessel carved from split wood symbolizes a government official serving special interests. How can it be compared to the sage who assists in governing without splitting? The sage does not divide the nation into conflicting factions by laws and orders, but rather embraces unity and harmonizes the nation as a coherent whole.

---

53 This verse is mainly from the WB edition. In the MWD text, the second and third stanzas are reversed. There, the second stanza ends with the symbol of "uncut wood," and the third with that of "the infinite." Since the last stanza is about uncut wood, thus the arrangement in the WB is more logical.

29

將欲取天下而為之，吾見其不得已。天下神器也，不可為者也。為者敗之，執
者失之。物，或行或隨，或熱或吹，或強或挫，或培或墮。是以聖人去甚，去
奢，去泰。

> If you want to take over the world and act upon it,
>> I think you will not succeed.
>
> The world is a sacred vessel.
> It cannot be acted upon.
> Those who act on it spoil it.
> Those who hold onto it lose it.
> Of things,
>> some move ahead and some lag behind;
>> some radiate heat and some blow cold;
>> some are strong and some are weak;
>> some are cultured and some are ejected.
>
> Therefore the sage avoids excess,
>> avoids extravagance, and avoids extreme.

COMMENTS

The reason that people tend to act toward extremes is because they
do not understand how duality functions. Cycles move rhythmically
between two polarities, as the rising and falling tides and the waxing
and waning moon. Such rhythms cannot be manipulated. Taoist tradition maintains that even Heaven and Earth cannot change this rhythm.
"The Great One Excretes Water" (appendix 2) states clearly that this
rhythm of nature is something Heaven cannot destroy and Earth cannot regulate. Indeed, Heaven and Earth cannot sustain a gusty wind or
a torrential rain for long (chapter 23). Therefore, it is important not to
fixate on the extremes.

Chapters 27, 28, and 29 are essentially on the same theme—embracing unity by respecting and accepting the different aspects of duality. In chapter 27, Lao Tzu illustrates that the sage cares about both the good and the non-good; in chapter 28, he relates the importance of harmonizing the opposites, and here in chapter 29 he reminds us that there is a rhythm in the ways opposites oscillate and that one cannot tamper with them.

30

以道佐人主，不以兵強於天下。其事好還: 師之所居，楚棘生之。善者果而已，
不以取強焉。果而勿驕，果而勿伐，果而勿矜。果而不得已，居; 是謂果而勿強。
物壯而老，是謂不道，不道早已。

> Assist your ruler in the way of *Tao*.
> Do not use military force to dominate the world.
> Matters of force are wont to backfire.
> Wherever the army has camped,
>   the field will be rampant with brambles and thorns.
> Those who are good accomplish only their mission.
> They do not triumph by force.
> They accomplish without arrogance.
> They accomplish without boasting.
> They accomplish without bragging.
> If they have no option to succeed, they abide.[54]
> This is known as accomplishing without force.
> When things are in their prime, yet appear aged,
>   this is not the way of *Tao*.
> What goes against *Tao* will perish early.

COMMENTS

Lao Tzu states, "If you want to take over the world and act upon it, I think
you will not succeed" (chapter 29). Here, he gives an example of what may
happen when one acts upon it by military force.

---

54   The words *abide* (*ju* 居) in this line and *is known as* (*shi-wie* 是謂) in the next are
     extra in the MWD text, but not in the WB edition. With the additional words, we
     read very clearly that these two lines emphasize what is meant by "accomplishing
     without force." However, without them, as in the WB, the two lines usually read,
     "They accomplish even without choice. They accomplish without force." Such a
     reading of the WB is obviously not as cogent as that of the MWD.

Many rulers know the dire consequence of war, but their ambition often overrides any humanitarian considerations. Lao Tzu warns that using coercion to achieve one's mission is against the way of *Tao*. The way of Tao is "not striving with others" (chapter 8). "Matters of force are wont to backfire" because every deed returns to its originator (see chapter 25). Those who hasten the demise of others only bring their own death earlier. Therefore, rulers who follow the way of *Tao* will not engage in such actions. They will use sincerity and humility to effect results. In history, there is a famous anecdote about the fourth Han Dynasty emperor, Liu Heng 劉恆 (r.180–157 B.C.E.), who succeeded in deflecting an imminent war by means of a sincere and humble letter to a general in revolt.[55]

---

55   See, for example, Nan, *Lao Tzu Ta Shui*, pp.14–22.

31

夫兵者，不祥之器也。物或惡之，故有欲者弗居。君子居則貴左，用兵則貴右，
故兵者非君子之器也。兵者不祥之器也。不得已而用之，恬淡為上，勿美也。
若美之，是樂殺人也。夫樂殺人，不可以得志於天下矣。是以吉事尚左，喪事
尚右。是以偏將軍居左，上將軍居右，言以喪禮居之也。殺人眾，以悲哀蒞之，
戰勝，以喪禮處之。

As for arms,
They are tools of ill omen!
Even creatures seem to detest them;
    thus, people who have desires avoid them.[56]
Sovereigns at home honor the left,
    at war honor the right.
Therefore, arms are not the tools of sovereigns.
Arms are tools of ill omen.
When people have no alternative but to use them,
    it is best to do so with detached calm.
People should not find glory in them.
Those who find glory in arms rejoice in killing.
Those who rejoice in killing cannot attain their will in the world.[57]
Celebrations favor the left.
Funerals favor the right.
The lieutenant general occupies the left,
    and the general occupies the right.
This signifies that war is conducted as a funeral.
Since so many are killed, it is befitting to be mournful and tearful;
    even a victory should be observed as a funeral.

---

56   These two lines also appear in chapter 24.

57   To attain their will in the world means to be leaders in the empire. Those "who have desires" mainly want to attain their will in the world. Unfortunately, they do not realize that leaders of the empire should adopt the will of the people as their own will rather than impose their ambitious will on the people (see chapter 49).

COMMENTS

The rites of observing the left and right sides may have been a custom in *Chu* 楚, where Lao Tzu comes from. He notes that, since war is conducted on the same side where funeral is conducted, and indeed there are so many deaths in a war, it is appropriate to observe even a victory as a funeral.

Lao Tzu urges rulers to refrain from waging wars, not only because the fields for livelihood are destroyed (chapter 30), but also, and more pressing, because of the enormous casualties in war (chapter 31). We shall see how he convincingly articulates ways to avoid war in chapters 65, 66, 80, and 81, and means to minimize casualties in war in chapters 67, 68, and 69.

32

道恆，無名。樸雖小，天下莫敢臣。侯王若能守之，萬物將自賓。天地相合，
以降甘露，民莫之令而自均。始制有名，名亦既有，夫亦將知止。知止所以不
殆。譬道之在天下也，猶小浴之與江海也。

> *Tao* is eternal and nameless.
> Though it is small like uncut wood,
>   no one in the world dares to treat it as a subordinate.
> When marquises and kings can abide by it,
>   the whole world will would flock to them as guests.
> When Heaven and Earth harmonize and bestow sweet dew,
>   without order, the people naturally share among themselves.
> Once legal systems arise, names follow.
> Now that there are names,
>   it is prudent to know when to stop.
> Knowing when to stop avoids danger;
>   it will be like the presence of *Tao* in the world;[58]
>   it will be like streams running into rivers and seas.[59]

COMMENTS

Lao Tzu states, "If you want to take the world and act upon it, I think you will not succeed" (chapter 29). He uses war as an example to show that those who want to dominate the world by force only hasten their own destruction. Here, he gives another example; rulers who control people by creating laws (names) are not going to succeed. This is against *Tao*, since *Tao* is nameless.

We may recall that Lao Tzu says, "A name that can connote fame is not the eternal Name" (chapter 1), and "From the present, going back to

---

58   This means, "No one in the world dares to treat it as a subordinate."
59   This means, "The whole world would flock to them as guests."

antiquity, its Name has never gone away" (chapter 21). Here, however, he says, "*Tao* is eternal and nameless" (chapter 32). What an oxymoron. Well, reading carefully, we understand: The name of *Tao* is eternal, yet it never creates any name (rule or law) to possess or control its creations (chapter 2); thus, it is eternal and nameless.

Tao is simple like uncut wood, which is never split. Those who govern by resorting to rules of reward and punishment are splitting the people into different competing factions. Lao Tzu observes that in ancient times, before such decrees are erected, the people related to one another harmoniously and would willingly share whatever is inherited from Heaven and Earth. When rulers stop creating laws, they naturally gain respect, as the presence of *Tao* in the world, and people will flock to them as streams running into rivers and seas. "Therefore great governing does no splitting" (chapter 28).

33

知人者智也，自知者明也；勝人者有力也，自勝者強也。知足者富也。強行者有志也。不失其所者久也。死而不忘者壽也。

> Those who know others are clever.
> Those who know the self are insightful.
> Those who overcome others have power.
> Those who overcome the self have inner strength.
> Those who are content are rich.
> Those who persevere have a firm will.
> Those who do not lose their bearing endure.
> Those who die but are not forgotten have true longevity.

COMMENTS

After many chapters on how to relate to the outside world, Lao Tzu returns to the theme of inner development lest we lose our bearing.

The "Tao Ching," which is book one of the *Tao Te Ching,* is near its end. We may consider chapters 34 to 37 its coda.

34

道泛呵，其可左右也。成功遂事而不名有也。萬物歸焉而不為主，則恆無欲也，可名於小。萬物歸焉而不為主，可名於大。是以聖人之能成大也，以其不為大也，故能成大。

> *Tao* spreads out everywhere.[60]
> It goes to the left and to the right.
> It completes its work and claims no name.[61]
> All things return to it,
> and it does not lord over them.[62]
> It is forever without desire;
> thus, it may be called small.
> All things return to it,
> and it does not lord over them;
> Thus, it may be called great.
> That sages can achieve greatness
> is because they never aim for greatness;
> so their greatness is fully actualized.

COMMENTS

In chapter 8, Lao Tzu states that "water," which flows to the lowest place, is close to *Tao*, but comes short of being *Tao* itself. Here, we understand why. It must be the order of magnitude, for *Tao* acts like a "flood," spreading out everywhere.

In this summary on the attributes of *Tao*, Lao Tzu offers a fresh view of smallness and greatness with regard to *Tao*. In chapter 32, he says that

---

60   The picture on this book's front cover tries to invoke such an image of *Tao*.

61   Cf. chapter 2: "They...accomplished without claiming credit."

62   Cf. chapter 2: "They...produce without possessiveness."

its simplicity is small like uncut wood. Here, he remarks that the non-possessive desire of *Tao* is as small as though nonexistent. Therefore, he owns nothing and controls nothing. In chapter 25, he states that *Tao* is so great that it seems to disappear afar, yet it returns from afar. Here, he describes its greatness in terms of its openness (receptiveness). It is so enormously open that it can accept all things.

In *The Lord's Prayer* (pp. 32–33), I use an elastic line as a metaphor for the smallness and greatness of *Tao*. We can imagine that when the line contracts to become infinitesimally short (small), it shows its non-possessive trait; when the line extends to infinite length (great), it indicates its receptive aspect.

As for sages, it is "because they are selfless that they are self-realized" (chapter 7). Similarly, it is "because they have never aimed for greatness, so their greatness is fully actualized" (chapter 34). This is exactly the effect of the persist–resist principle (chapters 22 to 24).

35

執大象，天下往。往而不害，安平泰。樂與餌，過客止。故道之出言也，曰「淡
呵，其無味也。」視之不足見，聽之不足聞，用之不足既。

> The whole world follows those who hold the great image;[63]
>> follows without harm
>> but finds in them security, peace, and joy.
> Music and food may attract passing travelers.
> However, it is said that what comes from *Tao*
>> is as bland, as without flavor.[64]
> Look, you hardly see it.[65]
> Listen, you hardly hear it.[66]
> Yet use it, you hardly exhaust it."[67]

COMMENTS

Those who master "heaviness and stillness" (chapter 26) automatically
hold the great image of *Tao*. Such saintly people are so secure and calm
that they seem to exude boundless joy. Food and music cannot compete
with the simplicity of such individuals. People would like to bask in their
aura and emulate their way of living.

---

63 Cf. chapter 4: "Its image precedes the Heavenly Lords"; and chapter 32: "When
    marquises and kings can abide by it, the whole world will flock to them as guests."

64 Cf. chapter 12: "The five flavors ruin the palate."

65 Cf. chapter 14: "Look at it, but see it not; we call it the 'invisible.'"

66 Cf. chapter 14: "Listen to it, but hear it not; we call it the 'inaudible.'"

67 Recall that the use of the vessel (chapter 4), the bellows (chapter 5), and the valley
    spirit (chapter 6) is inexhaustible.

36

將欲歛之，必固張之；將欲弱之，必固強之；將欲去之，必固興之；將欲取之，
必固與之。是謂微明，柔弱勝剛強。魚不可脫於淵，邦之利器不可以示人。

> When something is going to shrink,
>   first it must have expanded.
> When something is starting to become weak,
>   first it must have been strong.
> When something is beginning to decline,
>   first it must have flourished.
> When something is to be taken away,
>   first it must have been given.[68]
> This is little understood;
>   the weak will take over the strong.
> Fish should not leave the deep.
> The nation's sharp tools should not be on display.

COMMENTS

Some read the beginning four lines of this chapter this way: "If you want to shrink something, you first cause it to expand. If you want to weaken something, you first make it strong. If you want..." Such a reading by itself is not wrong, but its tone suggests that Lao Tzu is advocating crafty tactics that are completely out of keeping with his philosophy. Because he consistently inspires us to become innocent like a baby (chapter 10 and 28), to be simple like uncut wood (chapters 15, 19, and 28), and to embrace unity (chapters 22 and 28), it is inconceivable that he would teach us to become crafty in this penultimate chapter of the "Tao Ching." Lao Tzu is simply

---

68 These first four lines are about opposites. Compare the opposites discussed in
    chapters 2, 22, and 29.

stating obvious facts of nature: one pole always leads to its opposite. In chapter 42, he clearly states the alternate of the two poles: "Things may be depleted and then filled, or may be filled and then depleted." Most people probably observe that the strong dominates, but they may not realize that the weak will eventually overcome the strong. Thus, Lao Tzu points out this largely ignored side of events. In fact, sages favor neither the weak nor the strong, because they are not sentimental and have no preferences (chapter 5). They simply follow the way of *Tao* and do not create schemes (names) to control anything.

In chapter 32, Lao Tzu recommends ending the creation of legal systems. Here, he says legal systems are, in effect, sharp tools that should not even be displayed. He uses the symbol of fish and hook to illustrate his point. Fish naturally remain in the depths, but when there are hooks with bait, they may be tempted to leave the deep and thereby get caught. Similarly, by nature, common people are content to live simple lives. However, when there are sharp tools (legal systems) on display, they are tempted to contend, to steal, and to agitate (see chapter 3). Therefore, it is better to keep the sharp tools obscure and out of sight.

37

道恆，無名。侯王若能守之，萬物將自化。化而欲作，吾將鎮之以無名之樸。
鎮之以無名之樸，夫將不欲。不欲以靜，天地將自正。

> *Tao* is eternal and nameless.[69]
> When marquises and kings abide by it,
>   all things will develop by themselves.
> If during their development, desires stir,
>   I will calm them by means of the nameless uncut wood.
> Calming by means of the nameless uncut wood
>   will clear of all desires.
> When desires are cleared stillness ensues.
> Heaven and Earth will self-adjust.[70]

COMMENTS

We may label each of our created laws by a name and designate each of our desires by a name. In both cases, *Tao* remains eternally "nameless." Thus, a ruler who follows *Tao* creates no laws to control the people, but rather helps them to tame their desires. When the people start to stir with desires, simply bring them back to the state of uncut wood (primal simplicity).

It seems great teachers drink from the same spring of universal wisdom. Tenzin Gyatso, the Fourteenth Dalai Lama of the modern world, also uses the symbol of plain wood for the practice of stillness. He says, "When attachment is about to arise within you or you feel like getting angry with someone, do not do anything: Do not speak; do not think—remain like a

---

69 This line is a repeat of the opening line in chapter 32. The repeat may be deliberate, so as to emphasis the connection between "nameless" and "not displaying sharp tools." However, in the WB edition, this line is completely altered. It reads: "*Tao* always takes no action, yet nothing is left undone" (道常無為而無不為).

70 It means all things will self-adjust according to the way of Heaven and Earth.

piece of wood." He lists many common situations in which we can practice remaining as a piece of wood.[71]

We have just coursed through the enchanting "Tao Ching" and shall continue into the expedient "Te Ching."

☯

---

71 Tenzin Gyatso, *In My Own Words*, p. 88.

BOOK TWO
TE CHING

38

上德不德，是以有德；下德不失德，是以無德。

上德無為而無以為也。上仁為之而無以為也；上義為之而有以為也。上禮為之
而莫之應也，則攘臂而扔之。

故失道而后德，失德而后仁，失仁而后義，失義而后禮。夫禮者，忠信之薄也，
而亂之首也。

前識者，道之華也，而愚之首也。是以大丈夫居其厚，而不居其薄；居其實，
不居其華。故去彼取此。

> People of superior virtue do not worry about their virtue;
>> thus, they have virtue.
> People of inferior virtue fear losing their virtue;
>> thus, they do not have virtue.[1]
> People of superior virtue practice non-action[2]
>> and have no selfish ends.
> People of high benevolence act
>> and have no selfish ends.
> People of high rectitude act but have selfish ends.
> People of high propriety act but find no responses.[3]
> They stretch out their arms and force others to comply.
> Losing *Tao*,[4] people resort to virtue.

---

1   The word *Te* 德 can mean "gain," "success," or "virtue" (see notes in chapter 23). If we choose the meaning "gain," we can read these first two lines as "Superior gainers do not worry about gaining, thus they gain. Inferior gainers fear not gaining, thus they do not gain." Having virtue is a form of gaining something, therefore, the above translations are special cases of this alternate reading. However, since this chapter is about virtue, we consider the special cases more appropriate.

2   We stated in chapter 2 that the term *non-action* (*wu-wei* 無為) refers to the mind being still and not astir. The full significance of *non-action* will be carefully explored in chapter 43 and thence.

3   The word *act* in these three cases is used to contrast the term *non-action*. It refers to the mind of those who are astir. Consequently, their external behaviors create much ado.

4   Cf. chapter 18, "When the Great *Tao* recedes."

Losing virtue, people resort to benevolence.
Losing benevolence, people resort to rectitude.
Losing rectitude, people resort to propriety.
Propriety is the thin husk of honesty and trust.
It is the onset of disorders.
Foreknowledge is the flowery ornament of *Tao*.
It is the origin of ignorance.
So, mature people stay with the thick rather than the thin.
They rest in the substantial rather than the superficial.
Therefore, they disregard the without
    and take care of the within.[5]

COMMENTS

In part one, the "Tao Ching," Lao Tzu discusses the mystical and potent virtue of *Tao*, encouraging students to practice "stillness" to attune to *Tao*. Now in part two, the "Te Ching," he concentrates on the practical aspects of cultivating "stillness." His presentation of the material is of pedagogical significance. He understands that students first need to become familiar with the principles of *Tao* before they can put them to use.

Lao Tzu starts part two with this observation: Some never worry about whether they have virtue, and invariably they have. Some always fear they do not have virtue, and generally they do not. There is no need to wonder why, for we learned in chapter 23 that these are the phenomena of the persist–resist principle. However, knowing the principle only helps us to see the cause and effect of events. To be truly virtuous, we need the mind to be still and empty—in Lao Tzu's words, to practice non-action.

As mentioned in chapter 18, in ancient times, people were vaguely aware of *Tao* and used oracles or divinations to learn the guidance of *Tao*.

---

5   Same line in chapter 12.

They simply follow the way of *Tao* naturally and, consequently do not worry about whether they do or do not have virtue. "When the Great *Tao* recedes," people receive the guidance of *Tao* from within. Foreknowledge through oracles and divination becomes like the flowery ornament of *Tao* and no longer functions as guidance.

Those who cultivate non-action (stillness of the mind) are able to follow the inner guidance of *Tao*. They are virtuous because, like the ancients, they do not worry about whether they have virtue or not. On the other hand, those who do not cultivate non-action (that is to say, allow the mind to remain astir with desires) often fear losing their virtue. Gradually, four types of people develop: the virtuous, the humanitarians, the moralists, and the propriety enforcers.

In this chapter Lao Tzu articulates the importance of non-action (stillness of the mind). As mentioned in chapter 26, other cultural traditions also teach the practice of "stillness." Lao Tzu, however, coins the term *non-action* (*wu-wei* 無為) to facilitate the practice. Indeed, the whole book of the "Te Ching" is chiefly an exposition on this practice.

Let us now turn to chapter 41, which is related to the theme of this chapter. We shall resume chapter 39 and the regular chapter sequence afterward.

41

上士聞道，勤而行之；中士聞道，若存若亡；下士聞道，大笑之。不笑不足以
為道。故建言有之：「明道若昧，進道若退，夷道若纇，上德若浴，大白若辱，
廣德若不足，建德若偷，質真若渝；大方無隅，大器晚成，大音希聲；大象無形。
」道隱無名，夫唯道，善始且善成。

When superior students hear the way of *Tao*,
　　they practice it diligently
When mediocre students hear the way of *Tao*,
　　they vacillate.
When inferior students hear the way of *Tao*,
　　they laugh loudly.
If they do not laugh, it will not be *Tao*.
Hence, there are these established sayings:[6]
　　Discerning in *Tao*, you still consider it obscure;
　　Progressing in *Tao*, you still feel it regressing;
　　Smoothing in *Tao*, you still regard it as rugged.
　　High virtue is like a stream.
　　Great glory is like a disgrace.
　　Abundant attainment seems deficient.
　　Established virtue seems stolen.
　　Pure essence seems soiled.
　　A great square appears without corners.
　　A great talent blooms late.
　　A great voice rarely sounds.
　　A great image seems without form.
Tao may be hidden and nameless,
Yet it is this *Tao* alone that is good at starting and completing.

6　These sayings reflect ideas explored in chapters 8, 13, 14, 15, 20, 21, 28.

COMMENTS

Why are we studying chapter 41 ahead of chapters 39 and 40? First, let us recall what is mentioned in the preface. We said that the chapters are numbered sequentially in the WB edition, but are not numbered in the MWD text. For convenience, we use the WB numbers when referring to the MWD chapters. As some of the chapters in the MWD text are not placed exactly as they are in the WB edition, the chapter numbers in the MWD appear out of sync in three occasions. We encountered one such case in the three chapters 22, 23, and 24 (here ordered 24, 22, and 23). Now we encounter the second case.

Next, let us consider the five chapters 38, 39, 40, 41, and 42, which are close to chapter 38 (which we just studied) and 41 (the present chapter). It is obvious that they appear consecutively in the WB edition. However, in the MWD text, they are out of order as follows: 38, 39, 41, 40, and 42. If we follow the MWD text we should now be studying chapter 39. But when we inspect these five chapters, we discover that the three chapters 39, 40, and 42 are connected to a common theme about the attributes of *Tao,* while chapter 41, which is about learning and practicing *Tao,* is more closely related to chapter 38. Therefore we propose studying them in this alternate sequence: 38, 41, 39, 40, and 42.

We suspect that this alternate sequence might have been the original chapter order until some scribe inadvertently switched 41 and 39. Thus, for a certain period these chapters appear in the order of 38, 39, 41, 40 and 42, as shown in the MWD text. Later, another scribe probably discovered that, in such an order, chapter 41 breaks the connectedness of 39 and 40 and needed to be moved somewhere else. Instead of placing 41 in front of 39 (as it should have been), it was placed after 40 (perpetuating the confusion) as reflected in the WB edition. We consider our alternative a more satisfactorily reading than that of the MWD and the WB.

Now, let us now examine chapter 41. Recall that in chapter 38, Lao Tzu explains why some people have virtue in their life and others do not. He observes that people, according to their attitude and accomplishment, can be grouped into four categories. He indicates that cultivating non-action (inner stillness) is the best way to gain virtue. We can imagine that many people who aspire to gain virtue would seek instruction on the practice of non-action.

The goal of non-action is to be at one with *Tao*. So they have to learn and practice the discipline of *Tao*. However, when learning and practicing a discipline like *Tao*, beginning students may find it difficult to confirm whether they are illumined or in the dark, progressing or regressing, on a smooth or on a bumpy road. As the sayings indicate, *Tao* is full of paradoxes. Students must practice diligently without vacillation. Lazy students who cannot grasp the subtleties of the discipline may regard this teaching of *Tao* as absurd and unworthy of their effort. Thus, they laugh loudly at their moment of "epiphany."

Anthroposophy provides a deeper perspective on why inferior students laugh loudly. According to Rudolf Steiner, when people fail to understand a subject and wish to simply ignore it, they establish a barrier to free themselves from connecting with that subject. By turning away from the matter, they become more self-conscious and feel a kind of liberation and thus "free the astral body from gripping the physical body." This relaxation of the astral body entails the physical action of smiling or laughing. Therefore, laughter is the spiritual expression of human striving for liberation from something seen as unworthy.[7] From Steiner's teaching, we see that inferior students, owing to their ignorance and arrogance, laugh loudly.

---

7 See Steiner, *The Being of Man and His Future Evolution*. For more on the astral body and its function, see appendix 1 and comments in chapter 10.

39

昔之得一者：天得一以清；地得一以寧；神得一以靈；谷得一以盈；侯王得一以為天下正。其致之。天無以清，將恐裂；地無以寧，將恐廢；神無以靈，將恐歇；谷無以盈，將恐竭；侯王無以貴高，將恐蹶。

故貴以賤為本，高以下為基。是以侯王自謂「孤」、「寡」、「不穀」。此其賤為本耶？非乎？故致譽無譽。是故不欲琭琭如玉。珞珞如石。

> Of old, these attained oneness—
>> Heaven, through oneness, became clear;
>> Earth, through oneness, became stable;
>> gods, through oneness, became potent;
>> streams, through oneness, became filled;
>> marquises and kings, through oneness,
>>> became the norm of the world.
> Had they clung to the extremes,
>> Heaven would not be clear and might crack;
>> Earth would not be stable and might crumble;
>> gods would not be potent and might stop functioning;
>> streams would not be filled and might run dry;
>> marquises and kings would not be noble and exalted
>>> and might stumble.
> Therefore, the noble is rooted in the humble,
>> and the exalted is founded on the low.
> That is why the marquises and kings call themselves
>> "the orphaned," "the widowed," and "the destitute."
> They take humility as their root, don't they?
> Indeed, over-glorification brings no glory.
> Therefore, do not aspire to shine like jade
>> or clatter like stones.

COMMENTS

Chapters 39, 40, and 42 are to be read as a single unit about the nature of *Tao*. Chapter 39 discusses the oneness aspect, 40 the returning and yielding aspect, and 42 the creation aspect.

Here, Lao Tzu mentions, for example, that in antiquity Heaven, Earth, gods, streams, and rulers realized the oneness aspect. Their realization of oneness enabled them to become clear, stable, and so on. It was important that each entity embraces oneness and "avoids excess, avoids extravagance, and avoids extreme" (chapter 29). If Heaven were to disregard oneness and cling to the extremes, it might lose its clarity and crack. During Lao Tzu's time, none of these adverse scenarios—except perhaps, in the case of the marquises and kings—happened. It means that they knew how the oneness (of *Tao*) functions and avoided extremes. Taoists sometimes refer to the practice of embracing oneness and avoiding extremes as "the middle way."

From chapter 17, we learn that rulers gradually stumble and can no longer serve as the norm of the world. According to Chuang Tzu (*Chuang Tzu*, book 10), since the time of Huang Ti 黃帝 [8] (c. third millennium B.C.E.), there have been no real royal monarchs in the Taoist tradition. Supreme rulership decayed because, "when the Great *Tao* recedes, humanity and morality emerge" (chapter 18). The rulers no longer embraced oneness and became arrogant, splitting the nation with names (chapter 32). They may still call themselves the orphaned, the widowed, and the destitute, but their actions are no longer the way of *Tao*.

We reason that Lao Tzu is not really trying to restore the ancient system of government. He probably uses the marquises and kings of antiquity

---

8   Rudolf Steiner remarks that Huang Ti, who is an earthly incarnation of Lucifer, is "the source of inspiration for much ancient culture." (*The Influence of Lucifer and Ahriman*, p. 16).

as symbols for the ideal "king," the self-realized sage (see comments in chapter 25). In Lao Tzu's time, those humble sages likely may have lived among the orphans, the widowers, and the destitute serving as their role models without claiming any credit.

40

反者道之動；弱者道之用。天下萬物生於有，有生於無。

> To return is how *Tao* moves.
> To yield is how *Tao* functions.
> All things of the world arise from *you*.
> *You* arises from *wu*.

COMMENTS

In chapter 39, Lao Tzu emphasizes the oneness attribute of *Tao*. Here, he relates the attributes of its movement and function. *Tao* moves by returning and it functions by yielding. How does *Tao* return? "Continually circulating yet never tired, it can be considered the mother of Heaven and Earth" (chapter 25). How does *Tao* yield? "Produce and nurture; produce without possessiveness; rear without control" (chapter 10; see also chapter 2).

Although Lao Tzu states that all things originate from the revealing state of *you*, and that *you* arises from the non-revealing state of *wu*, it does not mean that *you* is not there when *Tao* is in the state of *wu*. It is for our reasoning mind that he mentions the two states in a linear way. Recall that, in chapter 11, he uses a wheel, a vessel, and a room as examples demonstrating the coexistence of *you* and *wu*. "These two appear together. They differ in name, yet are considered the same" (chapter 1). They simultaneously produce each other as "the have" and "the have-not" (chapter 2) .

42

道生一，一生二，二生三，三生萬物。萬物負陰而抱陽，沖氣以為和。人之所
惡，唯「孤」、「寡」、「不谷」。而王公以為稱。故，物或損之而益，或益之而
損。人之所教，亦議而教人：「強梁者不得死」，我將以為學父。

> *Tao* produces one.
> One produces two.
> Two produces three.
> Three produces a myriad of things.[9]
> All things bear the *yin*, embrace the *yang*,
>   and harmonize with a tuning energy [☯].[10]
> People mostly hate to be orphaned, widowed, or destitute.
> Yet kings and dukes call themselves by these names.
> Therefore, things may be depleted and then filled,
>   or may be filled and then depleted.
> The maxim that others teach, I, too, decide to teach,
>   "Violent offenders will die a violent death."
> I regard this to be the father of all learning.

COMMENTS

According to Lao Tzu, *Tao* circulates unendingly and continues revealing
and not revealing in the states of *you* and *wu*, which forever coexist as one.
In the revealing state, *You* splits into *yin* and *yang*, and a third harmonizing energy is produced. Thereby, these three energies create a myriad of
things. From this we see that *three* implies the possibility of plenty. Intui-
tively, we use *three* to imply a great deal. For example, we say, "Three is
a crowd."

---

9   See also chapter 25 and appendix 2 on the creation process.

10   For information on how this beginning passage relates to the *tai-ji-tu* (☯), see Sit,
     The Lord's Prayer, pp. 20–21.

Lao Tzu seems to say that one comes first, then two, then three, and then all things. In reality, they are inherent in *Tao*, coexisting always. It is only because we are confined in space and time that they have to be stated in a linear way for our comprehension. Thus, it is best to simply regard *Tao* as the all-inclusive one. Maybe this is why ancient Taoists called *Tao* the Great One.

Recall, in chapter 2, Lao Tzu discusses the dual nature of things without mentioning a middle third aspect. Here, he explains that, whenever there are two, a third naturally arises as an interface that balances them. Just as in time "now" connects past and future, in space "here" balances the three dimensional poles of left–right, up–down, and front–back. Thus, *three* is an inherent aspect of *Tao*. We may infer that Lao Tzu frequently uses triads on themes to implicate this attribute of *Tao*.[11]

Everything is always alternating between two opposite poles, which have no intrinsic values. People attach values to the poles only because of personal preferences. For instance, many like goodness and glory but detest badness and humiliation. Yet kings and dukes of antiquity did not mind calling themselves the orphaned, the widowed, and the destitute. They have great good like water, "nourishing all things" and striving "to settle in places where people detest" (chapter 8). They called themselves by detested names to indicate their immense humility and their lack of any desire whatsoever to control others.

Although Lao Tzu informs us that *Tao* transcends good and bad, he advises us strongly not to use violence. It's not that *Tao* abhors violence. Remember, "Heaven and Earth are not sentimental" (chapter 5). Where violence originates, violence *returns* (see discussions of returns in chapters 16 and 25). We reap what we sow. The reason that people do not see

---

11   To learn more on the meaning of three, see appendix 2 in this book and Sit, *The Lord's Prayer*, chapter 1.

violence *return* to its originator is probably because they cannot recall their own past actions (especially actions that date back to a previous life), nor can they foresee what may happen to them in the distant future. However, Anthroposophy informs us that people will gradually develop a form of consciousness through which it will be possible to understand the laws of karma. Then, when things happen to them, they may know that such events are the fruits of their own past thoughts, feelings, and actions; and when they initiate an act, they may foresee the future effects that may ensue as a result of their present seed of action.[12] Nevertheless, we do not need to wait for this consciousness to develop before heeding the maxim: "Violent offenders will die a violent death."

---

12   For more on the topic of karma and reincarnation, see Steiner, *Theosophy*, chapter
     2: "Destiny and the Reincarnation of the Spirit."

43

天下之至柔，馳騁天下之至堅。無有入無間。吾是以知無為之有益。不言之教，
無為之益，天下希能及之矣。

The softest things in the world gallop over the hardest things.
That which has no substance penetrates into that which has no gaps.
Hence I understand the benefit of non-action (*wu-wei*).
Wordless teaching and the benefit of non-action—
   hardly any endeavor in the world can compare with them.

COMMENTS

This chapter and the next five (chapters 43 to 48) are the beginning exploration of the concept of "non-action" (*wu-wei* 無為). Lao Tzu uses this term in chapters 2 and 38 without much elaboration. Here, he reveals what motivates him to coin this term. He explains that when observing the soft and the non-substantial overtaking the hard and the dense, he understands the advantage when "nothingness" (*wu* 無) is in "action" (*wei* 為). So he coins the term "non-action." He reasons that when we emulate the spirit of nothingness in all our endeavors we can also achieve powerful and effective results. Loosely speaking, "non-action" is to let the spirit of nothingness direct our actions. Lao Tzu first shows us the importance of cultivating this attitude of non-action in chapters 44 to 48 and then illustrates the practice of non-action in the rest of the "Te Ching."

Many interpret non-action as no action or doing nothing. We already stated in chapters 2 and 38 that the term has more to do with the state of the mind than with external behavior. Only occasionally it is used to refer to the manner of how a task is conducted, and in that case non-action means action without fuss. In such instances, we may replace the term non-action with non-ado, or action without fuss (see e.g., chapter 64).

Let us reverse the term, like flipping a coin, from *non-action* (*wu-wei* 無為) to a backward term *action-non* (*wei-wu* 為無, to act with nothingness) and see what we can deduce about the mind's state. To "act with nothingness" can be to act without one's ego hindering the process—acting with no selfish motives; acting without fussing over the eventual outcome. Just act without mulling over the factors that could interfere with the successful completion of a task. In other words, we keep our mind focused completely on the task with no distractions. When practicing "action-non," one's state of the mind is like the eye of a hurricane, completely calm and still, yet advancing powerfully. So "non-action" and "action-non" are like two sides of a coin, referring to the same state of a stilled mind.

In chapter 48, Lao Tzu creates another term *non-affair* (*wu-shi* 無事) which essentially means "action-non." Thus non-action and non-affair both refer to the state of a stilled mind, with great concentration on the task at hand. To emphasize this ideal approach to undertakings, Lao Tzu ingeniously creates terms by appending words to the prefix *non-* (*wu-* 無), as in *non-flavor, non-marching, non-enemy,* and so on.

44

名與身孰親？身與貨孰多？得與亡孰病？是故，甚愛必大費，多藏必厚亡。知足不辱，知止不殆，可以長久。

> Fame or body, which is dearer?
> Body or wealth, which is more precious?
> Gaining or losing, which is more afflicting?[13]
> Therefore, excessive craving incurs great expense.
> Extreme hoarding entails tremendous loss.
> Contentment avoids disgrace.
> Knowing when to stop avoids danger.
> Only then can we endure.

COMMENTS

Lao Tzu, the master teacher, reiterates the importance of not being excessive, which he has mentioned explicitly in chapters 9, 29, and 39, and implicitly in many other chapters. When we work and interact with others, we usually get compensated and become known. Thus, it is important for us not to get carried away and forget our root. It is natural to ask why some people can be content with who they are and what they have, while others cannot. Lao Tzu does not offer an answer here, but we should be able to conceive an answer after studying the next few chapters.

---

13 Cf. favor and calamity in chapter 13.

45

大成若缺，其用不弊。大盈若沖，其用不窮。大直如屈，大巧如拙，大辯如訥。
躁勝寒，靜勝熱，清靜可以為天下正。

> Great perfection seems incomplete,[14]
> > yet its use is never worn out.
> Great fullness seems empty,
> > yet its use is inexhaustible.[15]
> Great rectitude seems bent.
> Great skill seems inept.
> Great eloquence seems inarticulate.
> Agitation overtakes cool.
> Stillness overcomes heat.
> Being clear and still,
> > one can be the norm of the world.

COMMENTS

Lao Tzu explains the perils of excess in pursuing fame and wealth and
states that we can avoid danger by knowing when to stop. It is not easy
for some people to be content and stop, even when they know they should.
Perhaps such people have never attempted to calm the mind. They do not
know that stillness can help them stay in the center and avoid excess.

In chapter 15 we learned that the Taoist adepts naturally appear as
hesitant, watchful, courteous, yielding, simple, open, and opaque. Their
traits may shed light on why they seem incomplete, empty, bent, inept, and

---

14   In the WB, *ruo* 若 is used in all five cases, whereas in the MWD, 若 is used only in
the beginning two cases and *ru* 如 in the other three. Generally, these two words
are interchangeable and both can be translated as "seem" and "appear." It is not
essential to differentiate them.

15   Cf. chapter 4; "*Tao* is empty. Yet its use is... inexhaustible."

inarticulate, even though they have great perfection, great talents, great rectitude, great skills, and great eloquence. It is their true humility that guides their conduct. They are content with who they are. There is thus no need for them "to shine like jade or clatter like stones" (chapter 39). However, they are not aloof. They do not lock the door (chapter 27). They would offer help as needed. They know that agitation can ruin their calm and self-control. Thus it is important to be still and to keep desires and excitements at bay.

46

天下有道，卻走馬以糞。天下無道，戎馬生於郊。罪莫大於可欲；禍莫大於不
知足；咎莫大於欲得。故，知足之足，恒足矣。

> When the world follows the way of *Tao*,
>> even galloping horses can by used to manure the fields.
> When the world neglects the way of *Tao*,
>> warring horses have to be bred on the outskirts.
> There is no greater fault than craving.
> There is no greater disaster than discontent.
> There is no greater calamity than greed.
> Therefore, being content is always sufficient.[16]

COMMENTS

Being discontented and not knowing when to stop create only disasters
and calamities such as war. Lao Tzu points out that the real root of war is
none other than human greed and discontent. So, isn't it urgent to cultivate
stillness, nurturing contentment and taming greed?

The different uses of horses during times of war and during times
of peace was probably common at Lao Tzu's time. However, we may
also regard war and peace as a metaphor for our state of mind, with
the warring horses symbolizing our desires. When greed and discontent
are tamed, not only will the horses not run amok, but their manure
can be used to enrich our mind-field, allowing us to maintain our cool
and calm much more easily. But when we let our cravings run wild, one
desire will breed another. Hence, even the remotest corner of our mind
is infected with discontent. This state of turmoil is indeed like a war.

---

16   Literally, "Therefore, the contentment of being content is always sufficient."

If we are ordinary citizens greed may lead only to personal downfall.
However, if we are heads of states or big organizations, then greed will
bring great social suffering.

47

不出戶，知天下；不窺牖，見天道。其出彌遠，其知彌少。是以聖人不行而知，
不見而名，不為而成。

> Without stepping out of the door,
> > they can know the way of the world.
> Without peeking through the window,
> > they can see the way of Heaven.
> The further one goes out, the less one knows.[17]
> So sages know without traveling.
> They name without their appearance.[18]
> They accomplish without stirring.

COMMENTS

Lao Tzu informs us sages discern the guidance of *Tao* from within, not
from without. Suppose we can be like those sages who tame their desire.
We would be content that we can naturally "disregard the without and
take care of the within" (chapter 12).

---

17 The less one knows about the guidance of *Tao*.

18 They can name what desires are potentially present without waiting for them to
    appear.

48

為學日益，為道日損。損之又損，以至於無為。無為而無不為。取天下常以無
事。及其有事，不足以取天下。

> Learning accumulates information daily.
> Practicing *Tao* diminishes egoism daily.
> Keep diminishing until non-action (*wu-wei*).
> Being non-action, one can accomplish everything.
> We take any task of the world as non-affair.[19]
> If we regard them as affair,
>   we cannot tackle any task of the world.

COMMENTS

This chapter summarizes chapters 43 to 47. Lao Tzu contrasts the difference between learning a subject and practicing *Tao*. Those who practice
Tao diminish their selfish desire and greed bit by bit. Eventually, they are
no longer agitated by desire for fame and wealth. This state is called "non-
action" (*wu-wei* 無為). If the mind within is in the state of non-action,
then without we can take our tasks as "non-affair" (*wu-shi* 無事), acting
with nothing to hinder completion (see comments in chapter 43).

The practice of non-action and non-affair can help us become "people of superior virtue" and depart from being "people of inferior virtue,"
because the mind will be still, with no worry about "gaining or losing
virtues" (chapter 38). In the rest of the "Te Ching," Lao Tzu continues to
expound on non-action, systematically guiding us closer to *Tao*.

---

19 Some read this line as "Win the world as non-affair." "Winning the world" is also
a task of the world, so this reading encompasses that interpretation as well.

49

聖人恆無心，以百姓之心為心。善者善之，不善者亦善之，德善也。信者信之，
不信者亦信之，德信也。聖人之在天下也，歙歙焉，為天下渾其心，百姓皆屬
其耳目，聖人皆孩之。

Sages have no set mind.
They adopt the mind of the common people as their own.
They are good to the good.
They are also good to the not-good.
This is the virtue of goodness.
They are truthful to the trustworthy.
They are also truthful to the untrustworthy.
This is the virtue of trust.
For the sake of the world, sages continually absorb.
They mix their mind with the world.
People function as their ears and eyes,
    which sages use like innocent children.

COMMENTS

Lao Tzu explains what happens when sages have diminished their egoism.
They then adopt the mind of the common people. People like to be treated
with goodness and trust. Thus, sages treat everyone with goodness and
trust without differentiation. People not only like to be trusted but they
also especially dislike being cheated. Thus, sages will not lie to anyone.

Sages consider people in the world as their ears and eyes. Like innocent
children, they use their ears and eyes to learn about the world around them
and have no desire to control and keep the world for themselves. They have
the mystic virtue.

50

出生入死。生之徒，十有三；死之徒，十有三。人生生，動皆之死地，亦十有三。
夫何故？以其生生也。蓋聞善攝生者，陵行不避兕虎，入軍不被甲兵。兕無所
投其角，虎無所措其爪，兵無所容其刃。夫何故？以其無死地。

> When we exit life, we enter death.
> The companions of life are thirteen.[20]
> The companions of death are thirteen.
> While people are born with life,
>   all their activities lead them to the realm of death.
> They are also done by these same thirteen.
> How is it so?
> It is because people live too intensely for life.
> I have heard that those who know how to live well
>   avoid no rhinos and tigers on land trips
>   and don no armor in battles.
> Rhinos can find nowhere to gore them,
>   tigers can find nowhere to claw them,
>   and the weapons can detect nowhere to pierce them.
> How is it so?
> It is because they have no mortal spots.

COMMENTS

When sages mix their mind with the world, they learn that people like
a long and healthy life. Therefore, Lao Tzu points out practical ways to
longevity. We may compare this chapter with chapter 7, which is on the
spiritual meaning of an everlasting life.

---

20 The thirteen are the four limbs and the nine apertures, seven for the senses and two
for evacuations.

When we are born, our body is accompanied with thirteen apparatuses. Throughout life, we use these thirteen until death. How do these thirteen lead us from life to death. According to Lao Tzu, the reason is that people live too intensely for life. They use these thirteen excessively to eat, drink, exercise, and engage in activities such as smoking and the use of drugs, which may be detrimental to human health. Many consider these thirteen to be their slaves rather than their companions. How can people secure long life?

Many of the material lures that seem most satisfying are in reality no different from rhinos, tigers, and weapons waiting to hurt us. Sages have no mortal spots, because they are no longer tempted by material lures. They maintain a long and healthy life because they do not indulge in the five colors, the five sounds, the five tastes, and the pursuit of hard-to-get goods.

51

道生之而德畜之，物形之而器成之。是以萬物尊道而貴德。道之尊，德之貴，
夫莫之爵而恒自然也。道生之，畜之，長之，育之，亭之，毒之，養之，覆之。生
而不有，為而不恃，長而不宰，是謂玄德。

> *Tao* produces all things, and its virtue nurtures them.
> Substance takes form, and vessels are completed.
> Thus, all things revere *Tao* and exalt its virtue.
> Their reverence for *Tao* and their exaltation of its virtue
>   are not for rewards but spontaneous.
> *Tao* produces them, nurtures them, rears them, nurses them,
>   matures them, ripens them, fosters them, and shelters them.
> Produce without possessiveness.[21]
> Act without conceit.
> Rear without control.
> This is the mystic virtue.

COMMENTS

When sages are completely still, without selfish agenda, and care only
about the wellbeing of the common people, they cannot be ruined by
material lures and are able to practice the mystic virtue.

---

21 Cf. chapter 10; "Produce and nurture; produce without possessiveness; rear without control. This is the mystic virtue."

52

天下有始，以為天下母。既得其母，以知其子。既知其子，復守其母，沒身不
殆。塞其兌，閉其門，終身不勤。啟其兌，濟其事，終身不救。見小曰明，守柔
曰強。用其光，復歸其明，無遺身殃，是謂襲常。

> The world has a beginning,
>> which can be considered the world's mother.
> Recognizing the mother, you can know the sons.
> Knowing the sons and abiding in the mother,
>> even to the end of life, you encounter no dangers.
> Sealing the passages and closing the doors,[22]
>> even to the end of life, you won't have to struggle.
> Opening the passages and striving your affairs,
>> even to the end of life, nothing can help you.
> Appearing small[23] signifies clarity.[24]
> Abiding in gentleness signifies strength.
> Use the light[25] to bring back the clarity.
> It will leave you without calamities.
> This is called following constancy.

COMMENTS

No matter how eloquent a teacher expounds on the way of *Tao*, if students
do not practice diligently, they will progress little (chapter 41). It is essential that those who aspire to abide in *Tao* practice non-action with resolve
and constancy.

---

22 The passages and doors are the sense organs.

23 Cf. Ch 34, "It is forever without desire. Thus it may be considered small."

24 The mind becomes clear when it is no longer blurred by desires.

25 The light is the stilled mind.

Here, Lao Tzu provides guidance for practice. We know already that *Tao* creates the world and everything is its manifestation (chapter 42 and 51). Hence, we may consider *Tao* the mother and all the created things her sons. If we find *Tao* (the mother) invisible, inaudible, intangible, and too fuzzy and hazy to discern clearly (chapter 14), then we can study and observe the sons—the created myriad things—to gain access to her.[26] Indeed, like mother, like son; there must be similarity. The mother–son relationship can help us reach the mother via her sons. Once we ground ourselves in *Tao*, even rhinos, tigers, and weapons cannot hurt us (chapter 50). What dangers will there be?

Development in *Tao* is an inner cultivation. We need to remind ourselves that our sensory organs are meant only to know the sons, while the goal is to abide in the mother. If while going within we are distracted by the outside world, how can we be still? The perils of the superficial are like rhinos, tigers, and weapons. Therefore, always shut off outside influences. We achieve clarity by making our desires so small that they become nonexistent. We develop strength by being soft, gentle, and yielding. We use the stilled mind to return to enlightenment and to regain simplicity.

---

26   Rudolf Steiner, who holds a similar view, says, "Everything to be seen in the kingdoms of mineral, plant, animal, and in the physical human kingdom, everything that makes an impression upon the sense organs, upon intellect and intelligence—all these things are nothing but symbols of the spirit; and only one who learns how to interpret these symbols reaches the reality, the spirit" ("Calendar of the Soul," a lecture on his book of the same title).

53

使我介然有知，行於大道，唯施是畏。大道甚夷，而民好解。朝甚除，田甚蕪，倉甚虛，服文采，帶利劍，厭飲食，財貨有餘，是為盜夸。非道也哉！

> What I firmly know is that,
>   when walking in the Great *Tao*,
>   the only fear is of straying from it.
> The Great *Tao* is actually flat and even.
> However, people like tortuous paths.
> While the courts are well trimmed,
>   the fields are full of weeds,
>   and the granaries are empty.
> They[27] wear fancy clothing.
> They carry sharp swords.
> They feast to satiation.
> They display their excess of wealth and goods.
> They act like bandits flaunting their spoils,
>   not the way of *Tao*.

COMMENTS

In chapter 1, Lao Tzu makes a pun that the walking road (*Tao*) is not the Primal Wisdom (*Tao*). He is at it again, but this time he treats the Primal Wisdom (*Tao*) as a road (*Tao*) for our walk in life.

"When walking in the Great *Tao*, the only fear is of straying from it." One needs continually to be alert and watchful. This is why Lao Tzu says, "Established virtue seems stolen" (chapter 41). If we are not vigilant, we become easily sidetracked. Many of those court officials probably never bother to know this *Tao*, let alone worry about becoming sidetracked. They want to use their position only to take from the people. Bandits indeed!

---

27   The court officials.

54

善建者不拔，善抱者不脫，子孫以祭祀不輟。修之於身，其德乃真；修之於家，
其德乃餘；修之於鄉，其德乃長；修之於邦，其德乃丰；修之於天下，其德乃
普。故以身觀身，以家觀家，以鄉觀鄉，以邦觀邦，以天下觀天下。吾何以知
天下然哉？以此。

What is it that, when well erected, will not topple?
What is it that, when firmly grasped, will not slip?
Hence, your dependents will never cease honoring it.
Cultivate it in yourself; its virtue will be genuine.
Cultivate it in your family; its virtue will be plenty.
Cultivate it in your village; its virtue will endure.
Cultivate it in your state; its virtue will be abundant.
Cultivate it in the world; its virtue will be universal.
Therefore, examine the person by the person;
 examine the family by the family;
 examine the village by the village;
 examine the state by the state;
 examine the world by the world.
How do I know the world is so?
By this.

COMMENTS

In chapter 53, Lao Tzu observes that rulers who do not walk the way of
Tao behave much like bandits, leaving the country in disarray. How different the situation is when people know that "the greatest virtue is solely
to follow *Tao*" (chapter 21) and to diligently cultivate its virtue. Although
this chapter is about the practice of *Tao*, Lao Tzu ingeniously illumines
the practice without ever mentioning the word *Tao*. It is like drawing our
attention to the moon just by pointing at it.

In chapter 23, Lao Tzu states that even Heaven and Earth cannot make a gusty wind last all morning or a torrential rain a whole day. Then what "thing" can achieve such feats that "when it is well erected, it will not topple... when firmly grasped, it will not slip away," so great is its virtue that it receives long-lasting veneration? The answer must be obvious; if not *Tao* what else? *Tao* is so great and magnificent that we should cultivate it at all times, both individually and collectively. Hence, its virtue will grow in all areas truly without bound. Thus, individuals will fulfill their destinies as individuals, families as families, villages as villages, states as states, and the world as the world. Despite the fact that different entities have various missions to fulfill, they all can accomplish their own by practicing *Tao*.

55

含德之厚，比於赤子。毒虫不螫，猛獸不據，攫鳥不搏。骨弱筋柔而握固。未
知牝牡之合而朘作，精之至也。終日號而不嗄，和之至也。知和曰常，知常曰
明。益生曰祥，心使氣曰強。物壯則老，謂之不道，不道早已。

Those who are steeped in virtue can be compared to babies.
Poisonous insects won't bite them.
Fierce beasts won't attack them.
Predatory birds won't pounce on them.
Their bones are tender and their tendons soft,
    yet their grip is firm.
They know nothing of nuptial union, yet their sexual organ stirs,
    for their virility is utterly full.
They howl all day, yet their voice is not hoarse,
    for they embody perfect harmony.
Knowing harmony is constancy.
Knowing constancy signifies clarity.[28]
Hastening growth is harmful.
Using the mind to control the breath is exerting force.
When things are in their prime yet appear aged,[29]
    this is not the way of *Tao*.
Those who go against *Tao* will perish early.

COMMENTS

Suppose we are dedicated to the practice of *Tao*. Then we will acquire
great virtue as fresh and potent as a baby. Babies are so full of energy and
vitality that they can be active all day with no sign of exhaustion. They

---

28   Cf. chapter 52: "Appearing small signifies clarity."

29   These last lines are also in chapter 30.

are so innocent and harmonious with the environment that material lures (symbolized here by insects, beasts, and birds) cannot harm them.

Recall, in chapter 50, Lao Tzu observes that, when people use the thirteen apparatuses excessively to eat, drink, and so on, they lead from life to death. Here, he notes that those who use the breath to regulate the vital energy to prolong life may have the opposite effect of hastening death. That may be why those who meditate are taught only to observe the breath as a means to quiet the mind and not to control the mind or the breath.

Taoist tradition maintains that, through certain exercises, the body can indeed return to a state like that of a baby. However, in this chapter as in many others, Lao Tzu offers only generalities about practices without giving specifics. We have to remind ourselves that the specifics must be given orally by teachers who are certain of their students' purity of heart. Our goal is not longevity, but "fulfillment of the self." In this respect, Lao Tzu's teaching serves no less majestically.

56

知者不言，言者不知。塞其兌，閉其門，挫其銳，解其紛，和其光，同其塵，是
謂玄同。故不可得而親，不可得而疏；不可得而利，不可得而害；不可得而貴，
不可得而賤。故為天下貴。

> Those who know will not say.
> Those who say do not know.
> Seal the passages and close the doors.[30]
> Blunt sharp edges and unravel tangles.
> Soften brightness and merge with dusts.[31]
> This is called the mystic merge.
> It can be neither endeared nor alienated.
> It can be neither enhanced nor harmed.
> It can be neither ennobled nor despised.
> Therefore, it is the most precious in the world.

COMMENTS

Again, this chapter is about *Tao*, yet the word *Tao* never appears. *Tao* is so profound and subtle that our language fails to articulate its immensity and its mystic virtue. No matter how much we say, we will still miss pertinent points. This is why those who are aware of this fact keep quiet. Those who say probably do not truly understand what *Tao* is.

The first two lines of this chapter inspired the well-known Tang Dynasty poet Po Chu-I 白居易 (772–846) to compose a sarcastic poem on Lao Tzu. It says:

---

30 Similar line in chapter 52.

31 These two lines are similar to expressions in chapter 4.

Talkers are not as knowing as mutes.
These words I have heard from Lao Tzu.
If he himself was one who knew,
Why did he write a book of five thousand words?[32]

It seems unlikely that Lao Tzu would have been offended by this poem. However, let us imagine a student asking Lao Tzu to comment on it. To entertain his student, the old master might have replied, "The poet can say what he likes. I merely point *a Tao* to *the Tao*" (其言可, 吾道以道而矣).

In the beginning two lines, Lao Tzu simply reports on an intriguing phenomenon in the practice of *Tao*. He is not exhorting people to follow suit. Probably, those who know *Tao* and cultivate its virtue naturally keep quiet about their practice. However, those who are not sure of the *Tao* or are having trouble with their practice would likely discuss such matters with others.

To be at one with *Tao*, on the one hand, we have to immerge ourselves deep within and shut off all outer distractions. On the other hand, we have to emerge from the depths to blend humbly and gently with the world. Indeed, this practice is most precious and "is called the mystic merge."

---

32 "言者不如知者默, 此語吾聞於老君, 若道老君是知者, 緣何自著五千文."

57

以正治邦，以奇用兵，以無事取天下。吾何以知其然哉？以此：天下多忌諱，而民彌貧；人多利器，國家滋昏；人多伎巧，奇物滋起；法令滋彰，盜賊多有。故聖人云：「我無為，而民自化；我好靜，而民自正；我無事，而民自富；我欲不欲，而民自樸。」

Rule a nation by the normal.
Use arms as the abnormal.
Manage tasks of the world as non-affairs.[33]
How do I know it is so?
By what is shown:
The more taboos there are in the world,
    the poorer the populace becomes.
The more lethal weapons the people possess,
    the more chaotic the nation becomes.
The more arty and crafty the people are,
    the more frequently bizarre events occur.
The more swollen the legislation grows,
    the more robbers and thieves arise.
Therefore, the sage says,
    "I practice non-action,
       and the people transform themselves.
    I keep still and the people rectify themselves.
    I manage tasks as non-affairs,
       and the people naturally grow rich.
    I desire no desires, and the people naturally become
       as simple as uncut wood."[34]

---

33 Similar statement in chapter 48.

34 The passage is essentially one idea expressed in four slightly different shades.

COMMENTS

Some read the opening couplet as: "Rule the nation by straightforward means. Wage war by crafty or surprise tactics." Such a reading is at odds with Lao Tzu's teaching which encourages us to be innocent like a baby (chapters 28 and 55) and not to use force to dominate the world (chapter 30). This chapter is not about war but about how to manage the interior affairs of a nation. (Lao Tzu does discuss war strategies in chapters 67 to 69 where he advocates embracing the Three Gems—compassion, frugality, and humility—but no crafty or surprise tactics.) The use of arms here probably refers to the use of force controlling one's own nation. Such a situation is indeed abnormal.

Suppose rulers diligently practice the mystic merge: "Seal the passages and close the doors. Blunt sharp edges and unravel tangles. Soften brightness and merge with dusts" (chapter 56). The nation will then be naturally orderly and require minimal management. We note, however, that such rulers were rare in Lao Tzu's time (see chapter 17). Nations are often chaotic and rulers resorted to law and order to maintain control. Experience shows that taboos set to restrain the citizens in the name of orderliness eventually lead to even more chaotic reactions. Lao Tzu explains that wise rulers govern without much ado. They know, when people are left alone, they will regulate their own conduct. "Heaven and Earth harmonize, and they bestow sweet dew. Without any order, people naturally share among themselves" (chapter 32).

People will transform themselves without being told to do so, because guidance no longer comes from outside. The guidance of *Tao* has receded externally and is now hidden within us as our conscience (see chapters 18 and 38). We need only to be still and our conscience will prompt us to do the best according to the situation. Each individual, owing to one's background, bears a different worldview, and each event merits its own approach. Some activities will be benevolent in one case and detrimental in another. Laws and orders may address some issues, but they usually leave many others unresolved.

On the surface it seems as though Lao Tzu guides rulers toward managing their nations. But, on closer examination, we intuit that he actually counsels us to become wise rulers of our whole being (see comments in chapters 25 and 37). If we remain calm and still, we can accomplish our tasks efficiently. But if we allow the mind to become flooded by greed and let emotions dominate our will, we will run wild like warring horses. According to Lao Tzu, such a chaotic state is abnormal and would never have occurred if we had been practicing non-action or, in the words of the Dalai Lama, were "being like a piece of wood" (chapter 37). It is far easier to maintain a calm, stable state than to remedy a disorderly one. Therefore, it is imperative that we embark on the Great *Tao* at once.

58

其政悶悶，其民屯屯；其政察察，其民缺缺。禍兮，福之所倚，福兮，禍之所
伏。孰知其極？其無正？正復為奇，善復為妖。人之迷，其日固久！是以聖人
方而不割，廉而不劌，直而不肆，光而不耀。

> When the government is dull and dumb,
>   the people have abundance.
> When the government is keen and sharp,
>   the people are impoverished.
> Calamity is where good fortune rests.
> Good fortune is where calamity lurks.
> Who knows how things will end?
> Is there no normality?
> The normal reverts to the abnormal.
> The good reverts to the sinister.
> Long indeed have people been confused.
> Thus, sages square but do not cut;
>   have integrity without violating;
>   are straight but not indulgent;
>   enlighten but do not dazzle.

COMMENTS

The principle of ruling a state—whether a nation or the self—is to practice
non-action. Before using concrete examples to illustrate the principle of
non-action in the next six chapters (59–64), Lao Tzu recounts the main
points in chapters 56 and 57.

People will live contentedly and within their means when they are left
to themselves. However, when a government constantly legislates, it must
levy the people heavily to support law enforcement. In such instances, citizens may not only feel overly restricted, but they may also have difficulty

making ends meet owing the high taxation. Thus, some may revert to cheating or stealing, leading to greater disorder. This is why it is better to govern with non-action.

Do fortune and misfortune occur accidentally? Do good and evil arise at random? Recall chapters 22 to 24, where we discussed the implication of the statement, "When they [people] are at one with gain, *Tao* gains with them. When they are at one with loss, *Tao* loses with them" (chapter 23). We learned that it is we who create our own life experiences. When we keep fussing about without calming ourselves, we live only in chaos. Therefore, wise rulers never overact. If they are rulers of a nation, they will remain especially in the background. "The best leaders are barely noticed.... When their tasks are successfully accomplished, let the people say, 'They just happened to us naturally'" (chapter 17).

59

治人、事天，莫若嗇。夫唯嗇，是以早服，早服是謂重積德。重積德則無不克。無不克則莫知其極。莫知其極，可以有國。有國之母，可以長久。是謂深根固柢，長生久視之道也。

> In governing people and serving Heaven,
> nothing compares to being sparing.
> Being sparing, you begin service early.
> Early service means you accumulate an abundance of virtue.
> An abundance of virtue enables you to overcome all obstacles.
> Overcoming all obstacles means you have limitless ability.
> When you have limitless ability,
> you can take charge of the country.
> Caring for the country like a mother,
> you can endure long.
> This is called establishing deep roots and a firm foundation.
> It is the way to long life and lasting vision.

COMMENTS

"Governing people and serving Heaven" are the duties of kings and lords of the past. Metaphorically, they stand for the general responsibilities of a leader, whether of an organization or the self.

Essentially, the term *sparing* implies "frugality," as used in chapter 67. When people are sparing, they do not want to waste time, energy, or resources, and thus they value planning ahead or beginning service early. Lao Tzu enumerates the benefits of early service deductively: abundance of virtue, resourcefulness, limitless ability, taking charge of a country (whether of the self, a small firm, a huge organization, or a great nation). Now we need to be careful; we should take charge like a mother: "to produce without possessiveness, to act without conceit, to rear without control" (chapter 51). Only then can we establish a deep and firm foundation. Thus, we can last long. Yet we should not forget, "When work is done, to retire is the way of Heaven" (chapter 9).

60

治大國若烹小鮮。以道蒞天下，其鬼不神。非其鬼不神，其神不傷人。非其神
不傷人，聖人亦不傷人。夫兩不相傷，故德交歸焉。

Manage a great nation as you would fry small fish.
When *Tao* is used in ruling the world,
    even ghosts lose their spiritual powers.
Not that they lose their spiritual powers;
    their powers can do no harm to people.
It is not only that ghosts do no harm;
    sages also do no harm.
Because both are harmless,
    their virtues meet and coincide.

COMMENTS

Chapter 60 concerns the management of a nation's internal matters, while chapter 61 deals with the management of international affairs. Lao Tzu uses the term *great nation* mainly to contrast the terms *small fish* in this chapter and *small nation* in the next. We can view a "nation" as great as the whole world or as small as one individual or anywhere in between. The principle of management is always non-action (chapter 43).

In chapters 57 and 58, Lao Tzu discusses in detail why one must rule the nation with non-action. Here, he uses the art of frying small fish to help us grasp the gist of the practice. We know that all our actions reflect our state of mind. If we can maintain the mind with non-action, then we will manage tasks naturally with non-affair (chapter 43). Let us explore this metaphor in terms of the mind.

Recall that, in chapter 16, Lao Tzu suggests training the mind, with the goal to "attain emptiness to the far end" and "keep stillness in the deep bottom." Yet, we must note that the mind continually issues thoughts nonstop, one after another. Therefore, to "still" the mind does not mean to restrain it from issuing thoughts. Rather, when a thought arises, we simply observe that thought. We do not disturb it, just as we do not disturb the small fish in a frying pan. If we simply let the "thought" be, it will gradually go away (like a fish when it is done and lifted out of the pan). Soon the next thought will appear and we repeat the process. According to experienced meditators, the gap between one thought and the next can be extended indefinitely, as though the mind is in a state of "emptiness."

The virtue of sages coincides naturally with *Tao,* because sages never harm people. However, ghosts try to harm people by arousing temptations in the mind. According to Lao Tzu, if people maintain the mind as though frying small fish, then ghosts cannot harm them and the virtue of ghosts coincides with *Tao,* too. Therefore, we may understand that both virtues meet and coincide with *Tao.*

61

大邦者下 流也，天下之 牝也，天下之交也。牝恒以靜 勝牡。為其靜也，故宜為
下也。故大邦以下小邦，則取小邦；小邦以下大邦，則取於大邦。故或下以取，
或下而取。大邦者不過欲兼畜人，小邦者不過欲入事人。夫皆得其欲，則大者
宜為下。

A great nation is the low land into which all streams flow.
It plays the female role in the intercourse of world affairs.
The female always wins over the male by being still.
Owing to stillness, she naturally takes the lower position.
So when a great nation lowers itself toward a small nation,
    it gains the trust of the small nation.
When a small nation lowers itself toward a great nation,
    it gains the acceptance of the great nation.
Hence, either being lower to gain trust
    or being lower to gain acceptance.
A great nation wants only to embrace and nurture others.
A small nation wants only to gain acceptance and serve others.
Both achieve their goals by being lower.
And so it is proper for a great nation to remain low.

COMMENTS

After commenting on pan-frying, Lao Tzu now uses the image of mating to
show how great and small nations will relate to each other when the mind
is still and without egoism.

If human beings learn how animals mate and realize that, in mating,
the purpose of the female is to embrace and nurture her partner and the
purpose of the male is to be accepted and serve her, then mating will truly
be making love. Each cares only about the wellbeing of the other over the

gratification of one's own lust. If we stress this ideal in sex education, rape and sexual harassment may diminish greatly.

Lao Tzu indicates how one relates with another when egoism is annihilated—that is, when the mind is in the state of non-action. He uses the imagery of mating to help us see the virtue of humility over domination. Depending on our area of proficiency, we may play the role of a great nation or a small nation. In either role, laying low (being humble) facilitates the smooth completion of the matter. Small nations are usually intimidated by great nations, and great nations are often prone to arrogance and indifference. Therefore, it is befitting for great nations to make an extra effort to remain "low."

62

道者，萬物之注也。善人之寶，不善人之所保。美言可以市，尊行可以賀人。人之不善，何棄之有？故立天子，置三卿，雖有拱璧以先駟馬，不若坐進此道。古之所以貴此道者何？不謂：求以得，有罪以免邪？故為天下貴。

> *Tao* is the reservoir into which all things converge.
> It is the treasure of the good and the refuge of the bad.
> Nice words may be bartered.
> Noble deeds may commend esteem.
> Even people are not good; why cast them out?[35]
> Therefore, the coronation of an emperor,
>   or the installment of three ministers,
>   even with a tribute of jade discs on horse-drawn carriages,
>   is not as good as sitting still and advancing in this *Tao*.
> Why did the ancients value this *Tao* so much?
> Did they not say, "You find what you seek
>   and are forgiven your transgression?"
> Therefore, it is the most precious in the world.

COMMENTS

Having used the activities of daily life to indicate the importance of being still, Lao Tzu now illustrates how stillness helps us gain the priceless virtue of *Tao*, for which even an emperor's coronation or a premier's installment is no match. We have maintained that his teaching is not intended solely for rulers and politicians, but is also meant for ordinary people who aspire to "rule" themselves. This chapter confirms our view.

Lao Tzu instills in his students the importance of consistently culti-vating the virtue of *Tao*, so that they can become role models for others.

---

35 Cf. chapter 27: "Therefore, sages are always good at saving people, and never abandon anyone."

An important feature of the virtue of *Tao* is the protection of the non-good. Most people are willing to honor and affiliate with the good but are reluctant to protect the bad. Therefore, he states clearly that *Tao* is all-embracing and will forgive transgressors. Cultivating compassion toward all—both the good and the bad—is a very important theme in Lao Tzu's teaching. We have seen this idea hinted at subtly in many earlier verses (chapters 5, 8, 16, 27. 28, 32, 49), and we shall see it articulated even more clearly in chapters 73 and 74.

63

為無為，事無事，味無味。大小《多少，報怨以德。圖難於其易；為大於其細。
天下之難作於易；天下之大作於細。是以聖人終不為大，故能成其大。夫輕諾
必寡信，》多易必多難。是以聖人猶難之，故終無難矣。

In 1993, archeologists found a collection of Lao Tzu documents in
a tomb at Guodian, Hubei Province. The tomb was sealed before 278
B.C.E. and dates to earlier than the tomb at Mawangdui (MWD) by
more than a hundred years.[36] The collection, called the "Bamboo Slip
Lao Tzu" (BSLT), contains thirty-one complete or partial chapters of the
Tao Te Ching (one of which is chapter 63) and a manuscript titled "The
Great One Excretes Water" (*Taiyi Shengshui* 太一生水, see appendix 2).
Chapter 63 of the BSLT version is much shorter than that of both the WB
edition (above) and the MWD text.[37] The words within the brackets are
not present; only one word *gi* 之 appears. We first translate the long WB
version and then show how the truncated text reads.

WB

Act with non-action.
Manage with non-affair.
Taste with non-flavor.
In matters great or small, 《complex or simple,
    requite grudges with kindness.
Tackle the difficult while it is still easy.
Accomplish the great while it is still small.
For all difficult matters arise from easy ones.
All great deeds arise from small ones.
Sages never aim to do anything great.
Thus, they can accomplish great deeds.

---

36   See the preface, p. xii; and Henricks, *Lao Tzu's Tao Te Ching*, pp. 1–8.

37   Incidentally, chapter 63 of the two MWD copies are in pretty bad shape, with
many missing words.

Now, casual promises are seldom kept.》
Things taken lightly often turn out difficult.
Hence, sages especially regard all things as difficult.
So, in the end, they encounter no difficulties.

BSLT

為無為，事無事，味無味。大小《之》多易必多難。是以聖人猶難之，故終無
難矣。

Act with non-action.
Manage with non-affair.
Taste with non-flavor.
In matters great or small,
   《those》 taken lightly often turn out difficult.
Hence, sages especially regard all things as difficult.
So, in the end, they encounter no difficulties.[38]

COMMENTS

To compare these two texts, it befits to read chapters 63 and 64 together.
Then we note that the BSLT is more focused, while the WB lengthily
expands with ideas from chapter 64. Thus, the BSLT is more likely the
authentic version.

Let us comment on the BSLT text. We note that Lao Tzu often infuses
and stresses the spirit of nothingness with the prefix *non* (*wu*), such as *non-
action* and *non-affair,* which we already discussed in chapter 43. Here, the
new term *non-flavor* means we should avoid craving or loathing any particular flavor. We should not let any preconceived idea about the food interfere with tasting. When oriented in this way, we can be at one with what

---

38   See also Henricks, *Lao Tzu's Tao Te Ching,* pp. 48–49

we eat and know whether the food is beneficial or harmful to the body. Because we eat and drink so often, we have plenty of opportunities to hone this skill and become healthier.

Lao Tzu explains that those who cultivate attitudes such as non-action, non-affair, and non-flavor will find no difficulty executing any task. They will develop the good habit of early service (chapter 59). Whatever they do, they always give it their full attention. They naturally anticipate all possible issues and devise strategies to handle them. When we can execute our work as planned, we do not consider it difficult. Only when we experience an unexpected development in our work do we consider it difficult. This frequently happens when we take things too lightly. Thus, if at the start we regard all things as especially difficult, then we will encounter no difficulties in the end.

64

其安易持；其未兆易謀；其脆易泮；其微易散。為之於未有，治之於未亂。合抱之木，作於毫末；九層之台，作於累土；千里之行，始於足下。為之者敗之；執者失之。是以，聖人無為，故無敗；無執，故無失。民之從事，恒於幾成而敗之。故曰：「慎終若始，則無敗事。」是以聖人欲不欲，而不貴難得之貨，學不學，而復眾人之所過。能輔萬物之自然而弗敢為。

What is at rest is easy to maintain.
What has not erupted is easy to restrain.
What is brittle is easy to shatter.
What is small is easy to scatter.
Attend to troubles before they appear.
Organize things before they are in disorder.
A tree of arm's width starts from a seedling.
A terrace nine stories high starts from a soil piling.
A thousand-mile trip starts from your footing.
Those who fuss over things fail them.
Those who grasp things lose them.
Hence, sages fuss over nothing[39] and fail nothing.
They grasp nothing and lose nothing.
People at work, often fail on the verge of success.
Therefore it is said,
    "Being careful at the end as at the start averts failure."
Hence, sages desire no desires.
They do not treasure hard-to-get goods.
They learn unlearning.
They rectify what others have learned in excess.
They assist all things to maintain their naturalness
    and never dare to fuss.

---

39 Here we render *wu-wei* 無為 as "fuss over nothing" rather than "practice non-action."

COMMENTS

Lao Tzu reminds students that all matters evolve from small and easy to large and difficult. Therefore, it is better to handle matters before they become big and difficult. Many people procrastinate until the pressing end. Thus, when they work it is hard for them not to fuss or worry about being unable to succeed. The persist–resist principle (chapter 23) indicates that they will inevitably fail. On the other hand those who practice non-action, non-affair, and non-favor maintain a good working habit with early service. Thus, at work, even in the very beginning, they already regard matters as difficult and pay full attention without fussing over them (see chapter 63). Maintaining this non-fussing attitude until the end ensures success. Therefore, "being careful at the end as at the start averts failure."

Indeed, "hardly any endeavor in the world can compare with [non-action]" (chapter 43). We shall learn how to apply this practice, even to winning a war.

Before formally expounding on the topic of war strategy in chapters 67, 68, and 69, Lao Tzu again articulates, in the next four chapters (65, 66, 80, and 81), the ideal way to rule a nation, so that war can be virtually avoided.

Please note that chapters 80 and 81, the final chapters in the WB edition, are moved to between chapters 66 and 67 in the MWD text (the third deviation in chapter arrangements between the WB and the MWD). We consider this chapter arrangement in the MWD to be superior. Not only does this duo blend well with the themes among these several chapters (65-69), but, more important, by moving this pair away from the end allows the message in the last four chapters (76 to 79) to be more pronounced.

65

古之為道者，非以明民，將以愚之。民之難治，以其知多。故以知知邦，邦之賊；不以知知邦，邦之福。知此兩者亦稽式。恒知稽式，是謂玄德。玄德深矣，遠矣，與物反矣，然后乃至大順。

> The ancients who practiced *Tao*
>> did not use it to make the people clever,[40]
>> but to keep them as fools.[41]
> People become unruly when they are too clever.
> Instructing the nation to become clever robs the nation.
> Not instructing the nation to become clever enriches the nation.
> Understand that these two are verified measures.
> Being constantly aware of these measures signifies mystic virtue.
> Mystic virtue is indeed deep and far-reaching.
> It helps all things return
>> until they go along with the great flow.

COMMENTS

Too much cleverness leads people to unruliness because the adulation of talents stirs them to contend; valuing hard-to-get goods incites them to steal; the display of desirables causes them to agitate (chapter 3). Therefore, Lao Tzu suggests three alternate approaches for an orderly society, "Banish sagacity, discard cleverness, the people will benefit a hundredfold. Banish humanity, discard righteousness, the people will again be filial and

---

40 Cf. chapter 3: "Always keep the people from being clever and without desire"; and chapter 10: "In loving people and governing the nation, can you avoid cleverness?"

41 The word *fool* (*yu* 愚) connotes the picture of a simple person with no concern for worldly wealth and fame. Lao Tzu has used the word *fool* in this sense before: "Most people have extra. I alone seem to be left out. I have the mind of a fool, completely turbid" (chapter 20).

kind. Banish craftiness, discard profiteering, and thieves and robbers will disappear" (chapter 19).

By contrast, the ancients guide the people to realize the ideal of a fool. "Observe simplicity and embrace purity. Diminish selfishness and minimize cravings" (chapter 19). They teach not by words (chapter 2) but by their conduct. Their motto is "I practice non-action, and the people transform themselves. I keep still, and the people rectify themselves. I manage tasks as non-affairs, and the people naturally grow rich. I desire no desires, and the people naturally become simple as uncut wood" (chapter 57). Then all can return to the Primal Simplicity, as tributaries flowing to a river or into an ocean.

66

江海所以能為百谷王者，以其善下之，故能為百谷王。是以聖人欲上民，必以言下之；欲先民，必以身后之。是以聖人居上而民不重，居前而民不害。是以天下樂推而不厭。以其不爭，故天下莫能與之爭。

How do great rivers and oceans become the lord of a hundred streams?
By locating lower than the streams,
    hence they become the lord of a hundred streams.
Sages gain respect from the people
    because they speak lowly of themselves.[42]
They lead the people,
    because they place their status behind the people.
So even when sages become their superior,
    the people do not feel oppressed.
When they become their leader,
    the people do not feel frightened.
The whole world is glad to promote them tirelessly.
By not contending, no one in the world can contend with them.[43]

COMMENTS

When sages lead all things back to their natural state in the great flow, the great ones become humble and receptive, and the small ones attend devotedly to their duties. In chapter 61, Lao Tzu uses mating as a metaphor to illumine the virtue of humility. Now he uses the relationship of tributaries and great rivers or oceans to shed light on the merit of bowing oneself low.

As mentioned in chapter 64, we now jump to chapters 80 and 81 before continuing with chapter 67 and the remaining chapters.

---

42   They call themselves "the orphaned," "the widowed," and "the destitute" (chapters 39, 42).

43   Same line as in chapter 22.

小邦，寡民，使有什伯人之器而勿用。使民重死而遠徙；雖有舟車，無所乘之。
有甲兵，無所陳之。使民復結繩而用之。甘其食，美其服，樂其俗，安其居。
鄰邦相望，雞犬之聲相聞，民至老死，不相往來。

Manage the state with little fuss.

Govern the people with few rules.

Ensure that weapons are not used though plenty have been made.

Let people regard death gravely and avoid migration.

Even with boats and carriages ready, there is no need to ride them.

Even with a stockpile of arms, there is no need to display them.

Let people revert to knotting ropes for records,[44]

> relishing their food,
>
> wearing decent clothing,
>
> enjoying their customs,
>
> feeling secure in their homes.

Neighboring states may overlook one another,

> and the sounds of dogs and cocks may be overheard.

Yet, until death, the people do not run back and forth.[45]

COMMENTS

Many read the beginning lines as, "Keep the country small with few inhabitants." However, we do not think Lao Tzu favors small states with few inhabitants. Recall in chapter 60, when we explored his ideas of ruling a great state, we noted that "great" and "small" are relative. The word *great* is used to contrast something small. There are always great and small

---

44 In ancient times, people knotted ropes to keep records, using large knots for great events and small knots for minor affairs. Then because of war, there were so many things to record that writing gradually developed. Returning to tying knots in ropes as records symbolizes the cessation of war.

45 There is no war requiring them to run back and forth.

states just as there are always tall and short people. In chapter 61, he points out only it is proper for great states to keep a low profile when dealing with small states. Thus, there is no reason to suppose that he favors small states with few inhabitants.

Lao Tzu observes that, in ruling a state, "The more swollen the legislation grows, the more robbers and thieves arise" (chapter 57). He shows how the sages of old ruled: "They assist all things to maintain their naturalness and never dare to fuss" (chapter 64). The Sages' "mystic virtue…helps all things return until they go along with the great flow" (chapter 65). Here, he recaps this ideal way of ruling in the beginning two lines.

Sadly, during Lao Tzu's time, almost no rulers governed in this way. States, both great and small, were in constant turmoil. There were many ambitious rulers who wanted to expand their territories. Consequently, even those with no ambition for expansion were pressed to stockpile arms for protection, and the people were levied heavily to support the expanding armies. Wars became so frequent that the people found it hard to live a decent life and merely eked out a means to survive. They may have kept their personal effects packed so they could leave the country quickly when imminent army deployments were detected. They did not causally regard life lightly and love migrating to unfamiliar regions. They moved only because they wanted to avoid danger and possible death. We imagine they did not dare to dream about a utopian land such as Peach Grove.

The noted pastoral poet Tao Jian 陶潛 (365–427) wrote a story about a fictitious place called Peach Grove. One day, a fisherman accidentally wanders into this Shangri-la, where he finds well-tilled fields and nicely maintained homes. He learns from the residents that they have been living there peacefully for many generations without any knowledge of the outside world. They tell the fisherman that long ago their ancestors hid in

Peach Grove to avoid war. Their ancestors enjoyed the peace and serenity in that land and never returned to their former abodes.

Contrasting with the inhabitants in this Shangri-la, most citizens of Lao Tzu's time ate meagerly and wore ragged clothes. Perhaps, that is why Lao Tzu hopes that the people can obtain enough food and dress adequately. Migration is always on their minds, so how can they observe customs and feel secure? If all rulers were able to keep the peace, the people would not mind living simply without convenient mechanical supports. If neighboring states were not at war, they would have no need to run back and forth madly in battles.

Lao Tzu may envision such a day of great harmony...but it is truly unfortunate that no rulers heeded his advice. The dire situation among the nations urged him to write about war strategies.

81

信言 不美，美言 不信。知者不博，博者不知。善者不多，多者不善。聖人無積，既以為人己愈有，既以與人己愈多。天之道，利而不害；聖人之道，為而不爭。

> Sincere words are not flowery.
> Flowery words are not sincere.
> Those who know are not widely learned.
> Those who are widely learned do not know.[46]
> Those who are good own little.
> Those own much are not good.[47]
> Sages do not hoard:
> > what they do for others enriches themselves more;
> > what they yield to others rewards themselves more.
> The way of Heaven is to benefit without harming.
> The way of the sage is to work without contending.

COMMENTS

Chapter 80 depicts the inhumane condition caused by war, while this chapter reiterates the importance of being neither greedy nor contending and thereby eliminating the main causes of war.

Please remember that war is a metaphor depicting the conflict between any two entities, whether nations, communities, individuals, or even unsettling desires. Lao Tzu's teaching of non-action can apply to all cases.

---

46 *Know* means "know how to practice *Tao*." Cf. chapter 48, "Learning accumulates information daily. Practicing *Tao* diminishes egoism daily."

47 Those who horde are often tempted to amass more. This easily leads them to become greedy and commit evils.

67

天下皆謂我道大，大而不肖。夫唯不肖，故能大。若肖，久矣其細也夫！我恒有
三寶，持而保之：一曰慈，二曰儉，三曰不敢為天下先。慈，故能勇；儉，故能
廣；不敢為天下先，故能成器長。今舍其慈且勇，舍其儉且廣，舍其后且先，則
死矣。夫慈，以戰則勝，以守則固。天將建之，如以慈垣之。

> The whole world says that my *Tao* is great—
>> great yet not resembling anything.
> It is exactly because it does not resembling anything
>> that it can be great.
> If it had resembled something,
>> it would have long been insignificant.
> I have Three Gems that I hold constantly.
> The first is compassion.
> The second is frugality.[48]
> The third is not daring to be ahead of the world.
> Being compassionate, I can be brave.
> Being frugal, I can gain abundance.
> Not daring to be ahead of the world,
>> I can be the chief of all vessels.[49]
> Now, people abandon compassion but try to be brave.
> They abandon frugality but try to gain abundance.
> They abandon being behind but try to lead.
> This is death.
> Indeed, compassion enables you to win in battles
>> and be secure in defense.
> It is as if Heaven keeps what it would establish
>> within a wall of compassion.

---

48 Cf. "sparing" in chapter 59.

49 Cf. chapter 28: "When uncut wood is broken up, it may become a vessel. But when sages serve, they become the chiefs of all officials."

COMMENTS

We have learned that Lao Tzu shows great empathy for those who suffer in war (chapters 30, 31, 80). Though he is peace loving and an advocate of nonviolence, he sees the eventuality of war in certain unusual circumstances. It can sometimes be compared to the need of surgery for a sick patient. If war or surgery is sometimes inevitable, then it should be conducted in the least invasive way possible. To this end, he discusses war strategies in chapters 67, 68, and 69.

Although Lao Tzu speaks of war that is cruel and inhuman, he nevertheless utilizes this opportunity for a discourse on the virtues of his Three Gems: compassion, frugality, and humility. It is especially important that we practice these virtues during adverse times. Among the Three Gems, Lao Tzu singles out the virtue of compassion. It seems clear that the cultivation of compassion can engender the virtues of frugality and humility. When we are compassionate toward all, we consider everything precious and useful; thus we do not waste anything and are frugal. When we are compassionate toward all, we consider everyone precious and important; thus we gladly let others go ahead and humbly stay behind.

In chapter 7, Lao Tzu says that Heaven and Earth "do not exist for themselves." In other words, they are compassionate. Thus those who are compassionate are following the way of Heaven and Earth and can endure naturally as they do.

68

善為士者，不武。善戰者，不怒。善勝敵者，不與。善用人者，為之下。是謂不
爭之德，是謂用人，是謂配天，古之極也。

> Good soldiers are not aggressive.
> Good warriors do not get angry.
> Good winners do not confront.
> Good managers regard themselves as below others.
> This is known as the virtue of not contending.
> This is known as the ability of engaging others.
> This is known as matching Heaven—the ultimate of the ancients.

COMMENTS

To Lao Tzu, the reason for war is not to dominate the world, but to disarm
the aggressor. Soldiers are the bloodline of the army. They are the ones
who inevitably do the fighting. So the most important preparation for war
is to educate the soldiers and mid-level officers, avoiding unnecessary con-
frontations. The soldiers need to be calm and not aggressive. The officers
need to be humble when issuing orders.

Lao Tzu mentions that, in the remote past, an army considered "not
contending" and "humility" to be important virtues. His statement
implies that armies during his time no longer deemed these virtues essential. Maybe his teachings can revive appreciation of these virtues in the
military, hence reducing casualties in wars.

69

用兵有言：「吾不敢為主，而為客；吾不進寸，而退尺。」是謂行無行，攘無臂，執無兵，乃無敵矣。禍莫大於無敵，無敵几喪吾寶。故稱兵相若，則哀者勝矣。

Military specialists have a saying:
    "We dare not play the host, but willingly play the guest.
    We do not advance an inch, but gladly retreat a foot."
It means:
    marching as non-marching,
    stretching out the arms as non-arms,
    holding weapons as non-weapons,
    thus, we can meet the enemy as non-enemy.
There is no disaster greater than regarding the enemy as unequal.
Regarding the enemy as unequal may risk losing my gems.
When equally matched opponents meet,
    the merciful side will prevail.

COMMENTS

According to Lao Tzu the strategic attitude in war is very important. Our mentality should not be that of a host taking initiatives, but rather that of a guest waiting to respond to the enemy's movements. Those who take the initial step are the impatient ones. They are like the restless mind that cannot be stilled, and thus they are bound to blunder. We do not advance even an inch because we are not aggressive and are willing to retreat a foot to negotiate a peace settlement.

    When the enemy starts the maneuver, we shall respond accordingly. "Marching as non-marching, stretching out the arms as non-arms, holding weapons as non-weapons, thus, we can meet the enemy as non-enemy." The way to execute these military maneuvers is the same as to carry out our daily activities. They are to be done just as, "Act with non-action, manage with non-affair, taste with non-flavor" (chapter 63). Soldiers advance with focus, yet do not worry about victory or defeat. When they join in battle, they certainly have their arms stretched out and fight with weapons. However, they are not to be distracted by the eventual results of their encounter. They simply perform the task with focus. They let the spirit of nothingness (*wu* 無) infuse in all their undertakings (chapter 43). Thus, they meet the enemy as non-enemy.

Meeting the enemy as non-enemy does not mean regarding the enemy as unequal. Regarding the enemy as unequal may instill arrogance rather than humility. It can have the domino effect of losing the teachings of Lao Tzu's Three Gems. We should respect our opponent on equal footing and have mercy on them. We do not fight to destroy others but only to disarm. The goal is to reestablish peace.

Thus, we see the potency of non-action. When the mind is stilled and emptied of desires, even wars can be won.

70

吾言甚易知，甚易行。天下莫能知，莫能行。言有宗，事有君。夫唯無知，是以不我知。知我者希，則我者貴。是以聖人被褐而懷玉。

My words are very easy to understand and practice.
Yet no one in the world understands and practices them.
My words have an ancestry.
My deeds have a sovereign lord.
They are unaware of this.
Thus they do not care to know me.
Those who know me are few.
Those who follow me are even rarer.
Hence, the sage dons coarse clothing,
　　while keeping jade inside the bosom.

COMMENTS

Lao Tzu reveals a humane strategy to win in war. However, he realizes that war mongers will not follow his advice. He might have students, yet few fully grasp the subtleties of his teaching. They might find his teaching of *Tao* overly vague and lack the daily patience to diminish egoism.[50] They might find it difficult to embrace both the good and the bad, to be content and not to be stirred by desires, to stay lowly like water and not to contend. According to Lao Tzu, these are all easy to accomplish when we are willing to still our mind to non-action. What a pity that so few in his time cared to inherit his precious jade!

50　Recall the inferior, laughing students in chapter 41.

71

知不知，上矣，不知知，病矣。是以聖人之不病，以其病病也，是以不病。

> Knowing that you do not know is best.
> Not knowing while assuming that you know is sickness.
> The reason that sages are not sick
>   is because they are sick of sickness.
> Therefore, they are not sick.

COMMENTS

It is disheartening to learn that Lao Tzu's contemporaries missed such a precious opportunity to learn directly from him. Yet, what really saddens him is the mental sickness of the so-called experts, who are actually ignorant. They do not know that the virtue of a ruler is to practice non-action, to maintain stillness, to manage with non-affair, and to desire no desires (chapter 57). As high government officials, their ignorance and greed invariably cause the country great ills, which Lao Tzu examines in chapters 72 to 75.

72

民不畏威，則大威將至矣。無狎其所居，無厭其所生。夫唯弗厭，是以不厭。
是以聖人自知而不自見也，自愛而不自貴也。故去彼取此。

> When the people no longer fear your authority,
>   greater authority arises.
> Do not meddle with their dwellings.
> Do not harass their livelihood.
> If you do not weary them,
>   they will not become weary of you.
> Thus, sages know themselves
>   but show not themselves.
> They have self-respect but are not arrogant.
> Therefore, they disregard the without
>   and take care of the within.[51]

COMMENTS

When a country is ruled by greedy officials, heavy taxes are unavoidable.
When the people feel too much aggravation, they may rebel and topple
the government. To remedy, it is important that the officials diminish
their greed by pacifying the mind instead of chasing fame and wealth (see
chapter 12).

---

51   This line also appears in chapters 12 and 38.

73

勇於敢者，則殺，勇於不敢者，則活。此兩者，或利或害。天之所惡，孰知其
故？天之道，不爭而善勝，不言而善應，不召而自來，姍然而善謀。天網恢恢，
疏而不失。

> Bravery with daring can get you killed.
> Bravery without daring can keep you alive.
> Of these two, one seems beneficial, the other harmful.
> Does anyone know why Heaven dislikes certain people?[52]
> This is the way of Heaven:
>> it does not contend, yet it is good at winning;
>> it does not speak yet responds well;
>> it does not need to be called yet appears;
>> it may act slowly, yet its plans are perfect;
> As a net, Heaven is vast indeed;
>> its mesh may be coarse, yet it loses nothing.

COMMENTS

Let us inspect chapter 67 to see what Lao Tzu means by "bravery with
daring" and "bravery without daring." "Being compassionate, therefore I can be brave.... Now people abandon compassion but try to be
brave.... This is death. Indeed, compassion enables you to win in battles
and be secure in defense. It is as if Heaven keeps what it would establish
within a wall of compassion." From this we see that "bravery with daring"
means "bravery without compassion," while "bravery without daring,"
means "bravery with compassion."

---

52 The next line in the WB edition: "Even the sage finds the question difficult" (是以
聖人猶難之) sounds superfluous in the discourse. Thus, we follow the MWD text
and omit it.

Brave and daring people are those who use force against others. However, Lao Tzu warns that "violent offenders will die a violent death" (chapter 42) and that "bravery with daring can get you killed."

In chapter 42, we discussed the fact that where violence originates violence *returns*. *Tao* works like a bellows—air in, air out—or like the valley that keeps echoing. It just circulates the effects of our deeds around. "It may act slowly, yet its plan is perfect." The effects may take decades or even a few lifetimes to return. Yet, all of us reap what we have sown. Therefore, it is better to practice "bravery without daring." When we sow brave acts with compassion, we reap the fruits of compassion.

To shake us up, Lao Tzu poses a sarcastic question: "Does anyone know why Heaven dislikes certain people?" In chapter 62, he clearly states that *Tao*, and by extension Heaven, "is the treasure of the good and the refuge of the bad.... You find what you seek and are forgiven your transgression." So Heaven dislikes no one and protects everyone. We are each alone responsible for our own acts. Our conscience is the best guide if we can only be still and pay attention to its prompts.

Heaven does not contend and, hence, no one can contend with it. In this sense, it never loses but always wins. The way of Heaven comes and goes without our summons. It is "continually circulating yet never tired" (chapter 25). It is the great mother nurturing all things (see, for example, chapter 51). If we imagine *Tao* casts "Heaven" as a net, the net is vast indeed. By proportion its mesh may appear so coarse that it easily loses things. Yet it captures everything. "Even people are not good; why cast them out?" (chapter 62) We are all safe and secure under Heaven. To *Tao*, we are all precious.

74

若民恒且不畏死，奈何以殺懼之？若民恒且畏死，而為奇者，吾將得而殺之，夫孰敢矣？若民恒且必畏死，則恒有司殺者。夫代司殺者殺，是謂代大匠斲也。夫代大匠斲者，則希不傷其手矣。

> If the people never fear death,
>> why scare them with execution?
> If the people always fear death,
>> and those who commit offenses are executed,
>> who would dare to offend?
> If the people definitely always fear death,[53]
>> then there must be a permanent executioner.
> To kill in place of the executioner
>> is like chopping wood in place of a master carpenter.
> When you chop wood for a master carpenter,
>> rarely are you able to avoid hurting your hand.

COMMENTS

In chapter 62, Lao Tzu says, "*[Tao]* is the refuge of the bad…and [you] are forgiven your transgression." We may infer that there is no "permanent executioner." Some offenders may be unaware of this conclusion. Nonetheless, their behavior shows they are subconsciously uninhibited by capital punishment. We have noted that "violent offenders will die a violent death," because what goes around comes around (chapter 42). There is no need of an executioner, creating more violence. Thus, Lao Tzu lightheartedly teases the rulers, who insist on intimidating their people with execution: "When you chop wood for a master carpenter, rarely are you able to avoid hurting your hand."

---

53 This line is in the MWD text but not in the WB edition.

75

民之飢，以其上食稅之多，是以飢。民之不治，以其上之有為，是以不治。民之輕死，以其上求生之厚，是以輕死。夫唯無以生為者，是賢於貴生。

> Why are the people starving?
> Their superiors tax them too heavily,
>   so they are starving.
> Why are the people unruly?
> Their superiors fuss too much,
>   so they are unruly.
> Why do the people take death lightly?
> Their superiors demand too much of life,
>   so they take death lightly.
> When they have nothing to live on,
>   how can it be better to value life?

COMMENTS

Depending on which edition of the *Tao Te Ching* we study, we can encounter the word "superiors" (*shang* 上) from once to three times in this chapter. For example, in the MWD text, it appears only once in the second case; in the WB edition, twice in the first and second cases; and in a certain traditional edition, three times in all the cases. We deem the traditional edition renders a reading most close to Lao Tzu's idea. See comments below.

Recently, an expert on the MWD *Lao Tzu* illustrated how better insight into ancient scripts renders this chapter a very different reading. This took place during the announcement of a project to publish the whole collection of the MWD scripts. The expert explained that the word we regard as "taxation" (*shui* 稅) can be an ancient script for the word *road*. Using this new insight, he could read chapter 75 like this (paraphrasing):

The people are starving because they have too many ways to get food. The people are hard to rule because their superiors do not practice non-action. The people do not mind death because they chase too keenly for a good life. So those who live simply are better than those who live lavishly.[54]

The new interpretation of the word *taxation* and the omission of the word *superiors* in the first and third answers in the MWD text enable the expert to read chapter 75 in a significantly different way from the traditional perspective. It is fair to say that his reading of this chapter agrees with the general philosophy of Lao Tzu (see, for example, chapters 12, 20, 50, and 57). Nevertheless, the tone of such a reading does not seem to connect well with the current theme in the exposition. Chapter 75 summarizes the preceding five chapters (70–74), which are about the rulers (superiors) and the ruled. Thus the inclusion of the word *superiors* is appropriate in every case. By using the new insight of the word *taxation* to mean "road," we may read that the superiors use many ways to eat into the people's livelihood, which is essentially the same as heavy taxation.

We deduce a central theme threading through chapters 70 to 75. To wit, the rulers disregard the jade (teachings) of the sage (70), but sickly regard their ignorant views as good policies in government (71). Hence, they burden their people with heavy taxation (72). They do not know that the way of Heaven is compassion without discrimination (73) and mistakenly use execution as a deterrent for crimes (74). Their ruling brings many ills to the people: starvation, unruliness, and lost hope (75).

Lao Tzu shows that the ills of society arise chiefly from greed, which people are unaware can be tamed by the practice of non-action. To help anchor the practice, he ends the "Te Ching" with a few uplifting pointers.

---

54   http://news.xinhuanet.com/tech/2008-09/04/content_9769317.htm (09/26/10).

76

人之生也柔弱，其死也堅強。草木之生也柔脆，其死也枯槁。故堅強者死之徒，柔弱者生之徒。是以兵強則不勝，木強則折，強大居下，柔弱居上。

When people are born, they are soft and weak.
At death, they become hard and strong [rigid].[55]
When plants are alive, they are soft and supple.
When they die, they shrivel and dry.
So hardness and strength [rigidity] are companions of death.
Softness and weakness are companions of life.
This is why strong [arrogant] armies will not win.[56]
Strong [rigid] trees are chopped.
The strong and mighty abide in the low.
The soft and tender abide in the above.[57]

COMMENTS

These last four chapters (76 to 79) of the "Te Ching" serve as a coda of the whole exposition. Chapters 76, 77, and 78 focus on the dynamics between the strong–hard–excess and the weak–gentle–deficient, while chapter 79 reminds us to be compassionate like Heaven.

Lao Tzu ingeniously uses the newborn and the dead to contrast the weak and the strong, indicating that the strong will decay and the weak will grow. When the weak develop, they gradually become strong. Afterward, the developed strong ones have to make way for the next wave of

---

55 The word *strong* (*qiang* 強), depending on its context, can mean "powerful," "arrogant," or "rigid."

56 Cf. chapter 69: "There is no disaster greater than regarding the enemy as unequal. Regarding the enemy as unequal may risk losing my gems."

57 Cf. appendix 2: "The way of Heaven values weakness. It trims what is already complete so as to foster what is starting to grow. It smites the strong and subdues the hard so as to help the soft and the weak."

the weak to flourish. This cycle of the weak constantly replacing the strong is the way of nature.[58] Lao Tzu points out this dynamic without any sentimentality or favoritism.[59]

---

58   See chapter 36: "The weak will take over the strong."

59   See appendix 2 for a further exploration of this theme.

77

天之道，其猶張弓也。高者抑之，下者舉之，有餘者損之，不足者補之。天之
道，損有餘而補不足。人之道，則不然：損不足以奉有餘。孰能有餘而有以取
奉於天者？唯有道者乎。是以聖人為而弗有，成功而弗居也，若此其不欲見賢
也。

> The way of Heaven is like stretching a bow.
> The upper is pressed down;
> > the lower is pulled up;
> > the excess is trimmed;
> > the deficient is supplemented.
> The way of Heaven is to diminish the excess
> > and compensate the deficient.[60]
> The way of human beings is totally contrary.
> People take from the needy and offer to the affluent.
> Who can take the excess and offer as Heaven does?
> Perhaps only those who follow the way of *Tao*.
> Hence, sages act without possessiveness.[61]
> They achieve without claiming credit.
> Indeed, they have no desire to display their virtue.

COMMENTS

Lao Tzu is deeply innovative. Having illuminated the way of *Tao* in life
and death, he directs our attention to the art of archery. In ancient China,
archery was one of the six arts[62] that all students had to master. It is as

---

60 Cf. note 57, page 154.

61 These last three lines read somewhat like those in chapter 2, "Sages let all things
arise freely, produce without possessiveness, act without conceit, accomplish
without claiming credit."

62 The six arts: rites, music, archery, charioteering, calligraphy, and mathematics.

common as using computers in the modern world. Everyone understands the principle of diminishing excess and compensating the deficient. Yet how sarcastic that people frequently do the opposite. Where can we find people of *Tao* who are always willing to offer their extra? Perhaps it is not so easy, because such individuals hide their virtue and simply remain anonymous.

78

天下莫柔弱於水，而攻堅強者莫之能勝，以其無以易之。柔之勝剛，弱之勝強，天下莫弗知，莫能行。是以聖人云：「受國之垢，是謂社稷主；受國之不祥，是謂天下王。」正言若反。

> Nothing in the world is softer and weaker than water.
> Yet nothing can surpass it
>   for subduing the hard and the strong.
> Nothing can replace it.
> Everyone knows that the soft overcomes the hard,
>   and the weak overcomes the strong,
>   yet no one can put it into practice.
> Sages therefore say,
>   "Those who suffer disasters for the country
>   are considered lords of the soil and the millet;
>   those who suffer ills for the country
>   are considered kings of the empire."
> True statements sound paradoxical.

COMMENTS

People generally regard high positions as symbols of honor but somehow forget that high positions come with great responsibilities. Looking through history, how many can we find who have been truly worthy of their official titles? To Lao Tzu, the ideal leaders help overcome hardships of the country and "retire when the work is done" (chapter 9). They show great virtue like water: persevere through disasters yet not contending.

79

和大怨，必有餘怨，焉可以為善？是以聖人執左契而不責於人。有德司契，無德司徹。天道無親，恆與善人。

> After deep grudges are reconciled,
>> residual grievances cannot be avoided.
> How can this be considered good?
> Therefore, sages hold the left-hand tally,
>> but they lay no claim on the debtor.[63]
> The virtuous take charge of the tally.
> The non-virtuous take charge of the taxes.
> The way of Heaven is impartial.
> It is always good to people.[64]

COMMENTS

Lao Tzu observes that, even if people settle their rancor, residual resentment still lingers. It won't disappear, just as a scar remains after a deep cut. Therefore, sages forgive all debts and hold nothing against anyone.

Now we have completed our journey through the *Tao Te Ching*. We are grateful for Lao Tzu's exquisite exposition on the way of *Tao* and its virtue. We may not remember all the salient points of the whole trip. However, we may keep the messages in this coda as our motto:

---

63 One who holds the left-hand tally with the debtor's signature can lay claim on the debtor.

64 This line literally reads: "It always accords with the good people." Since good people are those who practice the virtue of goodness, they are good to both the good and the not good (chapter 49). Hence, we opt for a more liberal rendition to stress this impartial trait of Heaven.

Observe life and death to understand the cyclic nature of the weak and the strong. Trim the excess and compensate the deficient like bow stretching. Imitate water—be humble and contend with no one. Emulate Heaven—be impartial and benefit all.

Thanks to Lao Tzu.

APPENDIX 1
A BRIEF INTRODUCTION TO ANTHROPOSOPHY

Anthroposophy is a study of the spiritual world propagated by the Austrian philosopher Rudolf Steiner (1861–1925). He also calls his study "spiritual science," because he investigates the spiritual world with the same rigorous criteria with which natural scientists investigate the physical world. He wrote extensively and presented more than 6,000 lectures to explain how human evolution is related to the spiritual world.

Steiner taught that anyone who has fully developed the spiritual organs will be able to read the akashic record (the memory of the cosmos) in the spiritual world and learn how human beings and our planet Earth have evolved and will continue to evolve. He developed many meditative exercises to help students awaken their dormant spiritual organs.[65] Nonetheless, he frequently remarked that once spiritual facts have been investigated they can be understood by healthy human reason and ordinary experience. Therefore, it is not necessary to develop higher spiritual organs to understand Anthroposophy.

1. The Four Members of the Human Being

Steiner explains that each human being consists of four principles, or members: physical body, etheric body, astral body, and "I." Let us examine the similarities and differences among the human, animal, plant, and mineral kingdoms to better grasp the functions of these four principles.

---

65   For a discussion of spiritual organs, see Sit, *The Lord's Prayer*, p. 9.

First, humans, animals, and plants have physical bodies similar to the minerals. Second, these physical bodies are different from the minerals because they are alive, having an etheric (life) principle, which minerals lack. Third, humans and animals are "higher" than plants because they have an astral body, the seat of feelings, emotions, and perceptions, which plants do not have. Fourth, because human beings have an "I," or self-awareness (which, in general, animals lack), they are the highest. The "I" (or true self) enables humans to use the brain to reason and facilitate remembrance of past events. Our life experiences are impressed into the etheric body, but we need the "I" to access those impressions.

These four interconnected principles intricately influence and work for one another. For example, the organs of the human physical body work for all four members. To a certain extent, we can say that the mechanical organs work for the physical body itself; the glandular organs work for the etheric body; the nerve organs work for the astral body; and the circulatory blood system works for the "I."

Fundamentally, our etheric and physical bodies are closely knitted as a lower unit. Men have a masculine physical body and a feminine etheric body; women have a feminine physical body and a masculine etheric body. In this sense, all human beings are both male and female. The Swiss psychologist Carl Jung (1875–1961) intuited this and stated that a man's inner personality is female, the *anima,* and that a woman's is male, the *animus.*

Complementing the lower aspect, the "I" and the astral body are interconnected as the higher unit. Each night, something mysterious happens to us. When we fall asleep, the higher unit leaves the lower and returns when one awakes. After a day's work of feeling, thinking, and willing in the etheric and the physical bodies, the "I" and astral body become exhausted and need to replenish their forces in the spiritual world. During their absence, a substitute "I" and astral being of divine spirituality maintain our nervous and circulatory systems. In the morning, upon awaking, the higher members return with renewed vigor. Because the etheric body during sleep is not with the higher members, it contains no record of what has happened during sleep. Hence, most people (those who are not clairvoyant) have no memory of what happens during their sleep.

In ancient times, initiates, through meditation and the guidance of a teacher, could induce a sleep-like state, upon which the etheric body (together with the astral body and the "I") would pass out of the physical body. Such a sleep-like state is somewhat like a near-death experience. When awakened by the teacher after about three-and-a-half days, the initiates gradually recall their experiences in the spiritual world. Steiner explains that in our time, the etheric body is immersed so deeply into the physical body that it is not suitable to use that method for spiritual knowledge today. He suggested many other exercises for gaining spiritual knowledge, eliminating the need to draw out the etheric body.

Throughout life, the four members of the human being commingle during waking hours. During sleep, the higher unit leaves the lower unit and returns when awake. At death, the higher unit together with the etheric body discard the physical body and do not return. After death, the etheric body reveals the record of one's life as a great "tableau." The "I" reviews that record, in reverse order, for about three days, after which the etheric body dissolves into the cosmic forces. The astral body also dissolves into the cosmos after a purifying period. The "I" retains the essences of these two bodies and continues to develop until a new birth.

Please note that, when we say the higher members "leave" the lower members during sleep or at death, they do not really go anywhere. The spiritual world is the basis of the physical world, but it is veiled by our sensory consciousness. "Leaving" means that they do not penetrate the lower members, but penetrate the spiritual world instead. It is beyond the scope of this quick outline to delve more deeply into this profound topic. Interested readers can consult anthroposophic literature.

2. Development of Consciousness

According to Anthroposophy, we first had a very dim consciousness, much like that of the minerals. It has taken us eons to develop from dim consciousness to self-aware consciousness. Our consciousness has been evolving for a very long time and will continue to evolve far into the future. In esoteric terms, the evolution of consciousness is divided into seven "planetary" phases (or days), termed Saturn, Sun, Moon, Earth, Jupiter, Venus, and Vulcan. Please note that these esoteric terms refer to phases of the planet Earth, not the heavenly bodies they represent today.

The days of our week reflect this esoteric knowledge, reminding us of our past, present, and future evolutions. Saturday is named for "Saturn's Day," Sunday for "Sun's Day," Monday for "Moon's Day," Tuesday for "Mars's Day" representing the first half of Earth evolution, before the Christ event on Earth. Wednesday is named for Mercury's Day" (since Christ), Thursday for "Thor's Day" (or "Jupiter's Day"), and Friday for Venus's Day. Vulcan is not included in the weekdays.

During Saturn's phase of cosmic evolution, the spiritual hierarchies (whose names and special functions during Earth's phase are outlined in section 4) endowed us with the physical body. It consisted of warmth and was quite unlike the solid physical body we now have. Laws of the physical body were established and we developed a deep trance-like consciousness. The present minerals are entities that lagged behind with that trance-like (deep-sleep) consciousness of Saturn's Day.

During Sun's Day, the hierarchies added the etheric body to the evolving physical body. Intelligence imbues the etheric body, and we develop a somewhat dreamless, sleep-like consciousness. Plants of today are lagged-behind entities with the dreamless sleep consciousness of Sun's Day.

During Moon's Day, the astral body was added to the evolving etheric body and physical body. Human beings developed a consciousness like dream-filled sleep with feelings and emotions. Animals today are those that lagged behind.

During our present Earth phase, the "I" has been added, and we have been developing and shall continue to develop waking consciousness.

In future planetary evolutions, the three bodies will become spiritualized. During Jupiter's Day, the astral body will become "spirit self" (also called *manas*), and we will attain what may be called *Imagination* (psychic) consciousness. During Venus's Day, the etheric body will become "life spirit" (*buddhi*), and we will attain *Inspiration* (super-psychic) consciousness. During Vulcan development, the physical body will become "spirit body" (*atma*), and we will attain *Intuition* (spiritual) consciousness. These future stages of evolution are still far away. For now, it is pertinent to focus on the present Earth evolution. Please note that following each planetary phase a rest period always occurs before the next phase begins. Moreover, during the initial period of each successive phase, a recapitulation of the earlier phases always takes place.

3. Evolution of the "I"

We can distinguish the "I" in two parts. The higher self is known as the "Christ spirit," while the lower self is the soul. For most of us, the Christ spirit is only a seed or embryo during the present Earth evolution. It will manifest its full functions in future planetary evolutions. Our main task during the present Earth phase is to develop the soul. Note that we may speak of many different aspects of existence. Yet, when we refer to an individual, we do not distinguish the different elements. We always refer to the commingled being of body, soul, and spirit as the individual.

As stated, the three bodies—physical, etheric, and astral—were prepared long ago, during three earlier planetary evolutionary stages, and they continue to evolve. During the initial period of the present Earth evolution, human beings (with the help of spiritual hierarchies) recapitulate the three earlier developments to become vessels of the soul and to evolve further.

According to the functions of the soul, we can separate it into three elements that develop progressively, one after another, in the three bodies. The "sentient soul" in the astral body; the "intellectual soul" (or mind soul) in the etheric body; and the "consciousness soul" in the physical body. As the soul began its development, we gradually lost our direct guidance from the hierarchies of the spiritual world. This was probably the time when "the Great *Tao* recedes" (chapter 18), as referred to by Lao Tzu. With this development, we gradually became free-thinking beings.

Briefly, the sentient soul, which is the awareness of sensory experience, developed around 3000 to 800 B.C.E. The intellectual soul, related to our awareness of the experience between our being and thinking, developed about 800 B.C.E. to 1400 C.E. The consciousness soul, bringing awareness of objective reality of the external world in contrast to our self, developed around 1400 and will continue until about 3600. We summarize the soul development in this table.

ELEMENT	sentient soul	intellectual soul	consciousness soul
ACTIVE EPOCH	3000–800 B.C.E.	800 B.C.E.– C.E. 1400	C.E. 1400–3600
VESSEL	astral body	etheric body	physical body
AWARENESS	sensory	being and thinking	reality of outer world and inner self

Designating these times for the soul's evolution is simply a convenient way of indicating that a particular soul element is actively developing during each epoch. Indeed, each soul element begins to develop in seed form during the preceding epoch and matures in the subsequent one.

We are now actively developing consciousness of the outer world and the inner self. This may explain why human beings today tend to be so materialistic and egoistic. We have to know and understand the external world and the inner self thoroughly before we can transcend both and realize the Christ spirit.

4. The Spiritual Hierarchies and the Evolution of Earth

We now focus on the evolution of the planet Earth, which runs parallel (and is interrelated) with the evolution of human consciousness. We sketch only from the Saturn's Day to the present Earth stage. Please keep in mind that this information is gathered through spiritual investigations, not physical experiments.

Rudolf Steiner explains that there are nine hierarchies between the Trinity of Father, Son and Holy Spirit and humankind, and that the manifestation of the Trinity arose through the work of the spiritual hierarchies. The table lists the names Steiner used (with the traditional Roman and Greek Christian names in parentheses). In the column on the right are their manifestations during the present Earth evolution.[66]

1. Spirits of Love (seraphim)	lightning/fire
2. Spirits of Harmony (cherubim)	clouds/air
3. Spirits of Will (thrones/thronos)	solid matter
4. Spirits of Wisdom (dominions/kyriotetes)	life
5. Spirits of Motion (mights/dynamis)	chemical/sound
6. Spirits of Form (powers/exusiai)	light
7. Spirits of Personality (principality/archai)	fire
8. Spirits of Fire (archangels/archangeloi)	air
9. Sons of Life (angels/angeloi)	water

---

66 Adapted from Smith, *The Burning Bush*, pp. 556, 600.

During Saturn's Day, the Spirits of Will (3) were the principal hierarchy responsible for the "Earth" then. They poured the warmth (fire) ether over the planet. The other hierarchies were also helping and evolving during Saturn's Day. After their extensive work, a long period of rest ensued, like cosmic sleep. Earth was then awakened to Sun's Day, and the Spirits of Wisdom (4) became the principle hierarchy. First, all the hierarchies recapitulated their previous developments. During Sun's Day, new elements of rarefied light ether and denser air ether were added to the warmth ether. Again, a long rest followed the extensive activity of Sun's Day.

Next, Moon's Day evolution begins. The principal hierarchy was the Spirits of Motion (5), who added rarefied sound (chemical) ether and denser water (liquid) ether.

Present Earth evolution began after a long rest from Moon's Day. Rarefied life ether and denser earth (solid) ether have been added during this phase of development. The Spirits of Form (6) are the principal hierarchy during the present Earth phase, with the other hierarchies helping as shown in the previous table.

The next table shows the ethers active during the four planetary stages of evolution, with the newly added ethers in italics:

SATURN'S DAY	SUN'S DAY	MOON'S DAY	PRESENT EARTH
warmth	*light*	*sound*	*life*
	warmth	light	sound
	air	warmth	light
		air	warmth
		water	air
			water
			earth

In the beginning of the Earth phase, all the ether elements are in a chaotic mix. As the hierarchies recapitulate the three earlier planetary developments, with their forces cyclically moving in and out through the mixture, the ether elements gradually separate. From this chaotic etheric mixture, water ether is first excreted by the thrones (3), then air ether by the cherubim (2), and fire ether by the seraphim (1). The Spirits of Form (6) bring them into solid forms. While the Spirits of Wisdom (4) pour life ether into the forms, the Spirits of Motion (5) add sound (chemical) ether into them. Gradually, the Spirits of Age come into activity. They comprise the Spirits of Personality (7), and some lagged behind Spirits of Form (6). The Spirits of Age are responsible for human history. The archangels (8) serve as "folk spirits" (the spirits of nations and peoples), while angels (9) act as intermediaries between human beings and the folk spirits.

This is an overly simplified version of the Earth evolution, with numerous important details omitted. The bibliography offers sources for those interested in further study of Rudolf Steiner's descriptions of cosmic evolution.[67]

5. *Lao Tzu's* Tao Te Ching

In view of the long history of the Earth and human evolution, we can see where Lao Tzu (c. sixth to fourth centuries B.C.E.) fits into this time line. He lived during the first third of the epoch, when the intellectual soul was developing. He was probably aware of the human evolutionary stages and understood the potential traps in the development of the intellectual soul. People may rely too heavily on the brain and sensory organs and become arrogant. His *Tao Te Ching* inspires people toward humility. We

---

67 The most detailed of these resources is Rudolf Steiner's book, *An Outline of Esoteric Science* and his lecture course, *The Spiritual Hierarchies and the Physical World: Zodiac, Planets, and Cosmos.*

can awaken our cosmic nature through our senses from without, yet we must nurture our spiritual self from within. We need to balance these two activities to be authentic human beings.

APPENDIX 2

THE GREAT ONE EXCRETES WATER

In 1993, archeologists found a collection of Lao Tzu documents in a tomb at Guodian, Hubei Province. This tomb, which was sealed before 278 B.C.E., is older than the tomb at Mawangdui (MWD) by more than a century (see preface). This collection, called the "Bamboo Slip Lao Tzu," contains thirty-one complete or partial chapters of the *Tao Te Ching* (we have translated chapter 63) and a manuscript titled "The Great One Excretes Water" (*Taiyi Shengshui* 太一生水) after its opening statement. This collection was made public in 1998 and has attracted keen interest among scholars of Lao Tzu. They are intrigued especially by this particular esoteric document and have explored it with enthusiasm (see, for example, Ames and Hall, Henricks, and Tam).

My desire to unravel the mystery of life led me to study Anthroposophy, the *Tao Te Ching*, and, fortuitously, this particular document. I am fascinated by the affinity of the creation process presented in this document and Anthroposophy. I hope my dabbling in this material may attract others to produce more extensive and in-depth critiques.

ORIGINAL TEXT

The Chinese text is adapted from Henricks, *Lao Tzu's Tao Te Ching*, pp. 126, 129, and Tam, *New Thoughts on the Cultural Meaning of "Taiyi Shengshui."*

A.

太一生水，水反輔太一，是以成天。天反輔太一，是以成地。天地【復相輔】也，是以成神明。神明復【相】輔也，是以成陰陽。陰陽復相輔也，是以成四時。四時復相輔也，是以成滄熱。滄熱復相輔也，是以成濕燥。濕燥復相輔也，成歲而止。

故歲者，濕燥之所生也。濕燥者，滄熱之所生也。滄熱者，【四時之所生也】。四時者，陰陽之所生【也】。陰陽者，神明之所生也。神明者，天地之所生也。天地者，太一之所生也。是故太一藏於水，行於時，周而或【始】，【以紀為】萬物母。一缺一盈，以紀為萬物經。此天之所不能殺，地之所不能厘，陰陽之所不能成。君子知此之謂【道】。

B.

下，土也，而謂之地。上，氣也，而謂之天。道亦其字也。請問其名？以道從事者，必托其名，故事成而身長。聖人之從事也，亦托其名，故功成而身不傷。天地名字並立。故過其方，不思相【當】。【天不足】於西北，其下高以強；地不足於東南，其上【低以弱】。【不足於上】者，有餘於下。不足於下者，有餘於上。

天道貴弱，削成者以益生者。伐於強，責於【堅以輔柔弱】。

TRANSLATION

A: The Great One excretes water. Water in return assists the Great One, thus forming Heaven. Heaven in return assists the Great One, thus forming the Earth. Heaven and Earth [repeatedly assist each other], thus forming darkness and brightness. Darkness and brightness repeatedly assist [each other], thus forming yin and yang. Yin and yang repeatedly assist each other, thus forming the four seasons. The four seasons repeatedly assist one another, thus forming cold and heat. Cold and heat repeatedly assist each other, thus forming wet and dry. Wet and dry repeatedly assist each other. They form the year and complete the cycle.

Therefore, the year is produced by wet and dry. Wet and dry are produced by cold and heat. Cold and heat [are produced by the four seasons]. The four seasons are produced by yin and yang. Yin and yang are produced by darkness and brightness. Darkness and brightness are produced by Heaven and Earth. Heaven and Earth are produced by the Great One.

Therefore, the Great One embodies in water and moves with time. It completes a cycle or [starts it], [setting this archetype as] the mother of all things. It empties or fills, setting this archetype as the way for all things. This is something Heaven cannot destroy, the Earth cannot regulate, and yin and yang cannot form. A nobleman[68] knows this is referred to as [*Tao*].

B: What is below is solid and we call it Earth. What is above is airy and we call it Heaven. *Tao* is also its designation. May we inquire about its Name? Those who work with *Tao* certainly rely on its Name. So they complete their tasks and endure. When sages work, they also rely on its Name. Therefore, they achieve their deeds and suffer no harm. With Heaven and Earth, name and designation are established together. Yet looking over their activity

---

68   See note 46, page 56.

domains, we do not consider them [the same]. [Heaven compensates what is deficient] in the northwest, bringing down the high and the strong. The Earth compensates what is deficient in the southeast, bringing up the low and the weak. [What is deficient in the above] has excess in the below. What is deficient in the below has excess in the above.

The way of Heaven values weakness. It trims what is already complete so as to foster what is starting to grow. It smites the strong and subdues [the hard so as to help the soft and the weak.]

COMMENTS ON TEXT A

Text A describes how the Great One initiates the creation process and the meaning of *Tao*. Text B explains the function of *Tao*.

When we compare the creation process stated in A with what is said about the Earth phase in Anthroposophy (appendix 1), we cannot help being amazed at their proximity. Now, let us see how the creation process stated in Text A correlates with the *Tao Te Ching* proper.

Recall that, in chapters 25 and 42, Lao Tzu briefly introduces the general creation process as follows:

There is something undifferentiated yet complete. It exists even before Heaven and Earth. Silent and boundless, standing alone and unchanging, continually circulating yet never tired, it can be considered the mother of Heaven and Earth. I do not yet know its name and refer to it as "*Tao*." If it must be named, I shall call it "Great." (chapter 25)

Tao produces one. One produces two. Two produces three. Three produces a myriad of things. All things bear the yin, embrace the yang, and harmonize with a tuning energy. (chapter 42)

The cyclic nature of *Tao* is emphasized in chapter 25, while the concept of three is stressed in chapter 42. The newly found document provides greater detail in the creation process and synthesizes the processes expressed in both chapters.

Chapter 25 mentions that in the beginning the Great One, existing before Heaven and Earth, keeps moving around. This document states that water first appears, and then Heaven and Earth are formed. They are formed through water that the Great One excretes. We should not regard this "water" element as physical H_2O water, but rather as primal matter in a fluid form. In Anthroposophy, it is called the "water ether." It gradually separates, forming Heaven and Earth. This is the first level of creation. There are three primal elements: water, heaven, and earth.

Chapter 42 states that three produces all things without much elaboration. This document states how the three primal elements help the Great One create the second triad of primal energies: darkness/brightness, yin/yang, and the four seasons. Continuing the process, the second triad helps form the third triad: cold/heat, wet/dry, and the year. The year is the end product in the creation cycle. Thus, we can take it that "three" symbolizes either the three primal elements or the three triads of primal energies. In addition, we can infer that, between each pair of the primal energies (brightness/darkness, yin/yang, cold/heat, and wet/dry), there is always a third interfacing energy balancing the pair. For example, chapter 42 mentions a third tuning energy harmonizing the yin and the yang.

The Great One starts a cycle excreting water and ends it with the "year," which is produced by a form of water (wet/dry). Therefore, we may consider that it embodies in water.

The terms *four seasons* and *year* both implicate the concept of time, yet they must signify certain differences. *Four seasons* probably represents the four energy principles as delineated in the Chien hexagram of the *I-Ching:* generating, prospering, benefiting, and persevering.[69] On

---

69   For a brief comment on the Chien hexagram, see Sit, *The Lord's Prayer* (p. 58).

the other hand, it is likely that the term *year* refers to some "Year-gods" whose function is to manage human affairs, much like the Spirits of Age in anthroposophic teachings. Indeed, the Chinese tradition speaks of sixty "Year-gods" (called the *tai-sui* 太歲), each of which is in charge of human affairs for one lunar year.

We can sketch this creation process in the form of three triangles arranged together. The composite figure has the prototype of the fractal Sierpinski triangle.[70] In this sense, the modern fractal concept is really old wine in a new bottle.

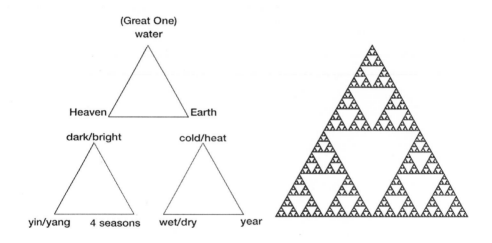

Triangles of Creation and Sierpinski Triangle

Finally, let us cite the passage on creation from Genesis in the Bible. We shall see that both documents also follow a strikingly similar course in their descriptions:

---

70 For an exploration of Sierpinski triangle as a model of *Tao*, see Sit, *The Lord's Prayer*, pp 16–32.

In the beginning God created the heavens and the Earth...and the Spirit of God was moving over the face of the waters....God separated the light from the darkness...and let the dry land appear.... And God said,... "Let there be lights...let them be for signs and for seasons and for days and years." (Genesis 1:1–14)

Please note that the Bible depicts the process with greater detail, while this extract contains only a few relevant points for comparison. In lecture 1 of *Genesis: Secrets of Creation*, Steiner mentions that those who wrote the Bible were very advanced seers of the spiritual world. This bamboo manuscript attests that during antiquity the Taoists were as highly accomplished. We also note that only Text A names the *yin* and *yang* energy, which neither Anthroposophy nor the Bible mentions.

COMMENTS ON TEXT B

Text B is about the way of *Tao*. We know from text A that the Great One excretes water. Water condenses below to form the solid earth. Anthroposophy teaches that this is the result of the function of the Spirits of Forms (see page 169). Water evaporates above to form the airy heavens. What we call Heaven and Earth are manifestations of the Great One through which it functions. The function of the Great One is called *Tao*. Loosely speaking, we also designate the functions of Heaven and Earth as *Tao*. This signifies that Heaven and Earth always act in the name (way) of *Tao*. Thus, when people act in the name (way) of *Tao,* they can also succeed and endure as Heaven and Earth do, without any harm.

We refer to Heaven and Earth together as *Tao*, yet their domains of activity are not the same. We shall infer that Lao Tzu (it does not matter whether "Lao Tzu" is the actual author of this document, since any ancient Taoist adept is undoubtedly conversant with this material) implicitly reveals the way of Heaven and Earth by means of the waning and waxing moon. This implicit use of the Moon can also be found in the Kun hexagram of the *I-Ching*, which says, "The southeast is beneficial for gaining friends, the northwest for losing friends." Here, "gaining friends" symbolizes the waxing Moon, and "losing friends" the waning Moon.

Let us consider the moon phases to see the way of Heaven and Earth. In the middle of a lunar month, the moon appears high in the sky with full brightness and lacks lowness and darkness. Heaven causes it to set and wane in the northwest,[71] compensating what it lacks. On the other hand, in the beginning of a lunar month, the new moon appears low in the horizon with complete darkness and lacking height and brightness. Earth causes it to rise and wax in the southeast,[72] compensating what it lacks. From the observation of these moon phases, Taoists opine that what is deficient in the above (namely, darkness and lowness) is excessive in the below. Conversely, what is deficient in the below (namely, brightness and height) is excessive in the above. Heaven and Earth may act in different directions, yet the principles of their actions are not different. Their way is to trim the excessive and foster the deficient.

We have to understand that to trim the excess, to smite the strong and to subdue the hard, transcends good and bad—or rather, are ultimately good. If the excess, the strong, and the hard are not annihilated, then the deficient, the weak, and the soft cannot develop. This is why it is said, "Heaven and Earth are not sentimental. They regard all things as straw dogs" (chapter 5). *Tao* operates in cycles. There is a time for germinating and growing and there is a time for declining and dying. This is the way of Heaven and Earth. This is the way of *Tao*.

---

71 This moon phase happens in winter in the Northern hemisphere. Directions are different in the Southern hemisphere and in other seasons. See the third table in http://curious.astro.cornell.edu/question.php?number=642 (09/26/10).

72 Ibid.

Recall that, in chapter 77, Lao Tzu uses the metaphor of a bow stretching to illustrate that the way of Heaven is to diminish the extra and compensate the deficient. This recently found document indeed confirms and exemplifies this teaching of the *Tao Te Ching*.

SELECTED BIBLIOGRAPHY

Ames, Roger T., and David L. Hall. *Dao De Jing: "Making This Life Signifi-cant": A Philosophical Translation*, New York: Ballantine, 2003.

Bynner, Witter. *The Way of Life: According to Lao Tzu: The Chinese Transla-tions*, New York: Farrar, Straus, and Giroux, 1978.

Chan, Hen-Shui 陳限水. *Lao Tzu Du Ben* 老子讀本, Tai Nam: Tai Xia Publish-ing, 1985.

Chang-Ren 常人. *Electronic Dao De Jing Jie* 道德經解電子版 (http://www.angeli-brary.com/oldies/daodejing.html, 09/26/10).

Chen, Cheng-Yih 程貞一. *Early Chinese Work in Natural Science: A Re-exam-ination of the Physics of Motion, Acoustics, Astronomy and Scientific Thoughts*, Hong Kong: Hong Kong University Press, 1996.

Chen, Ellen M. *The Tao Te Ching: A New Translation with Commentary*, New York: Paragon House, 1989.

Chödrön, Pema. *The Wisdom of No Escape and the Path of Loving-Kindness*, Boston: Shambhala, 2001.

Dale, Ralph Alan. *Tao Te Ching: A New Translation & Commentary*, London: Watkins, 2002.

Feng, Gia-Fu, and Jane English. *Lao Tzu Tao Te Ching* (25th-anniversary ed.), New York: Vintage, 1997.

Grigg, Ray. *The New Lao Tzu: A Contemporary Tao Te Ching*, Boston: Tuttle, 1995.

Gyatso, Tensin (The 14th Dalai Lama). *In My own Words: An Introduction to My Teachings and Philosophy*, Carlsbad, CA: Hay House, 2008.

Hamill, Sam. *Tao Te Ching: A New Translation*, Boston: Shambhala, 2007.

Henricks, Robert G. *Lao-Tzu Te-Tao Ching: A New Translation Based on the Recently Discovered Ma-wang-tui Texts*, New York: Ballatine Books, 1989.

————. *Lao Tzu's Tao Te Ching: A Translation of the Startling New Documents Found at Guodian*, New York: Columbia University Press, 2000.

Hinton, David. *Tao Te Ching: Lao Tzu*, Washington, DC: Counterpoint, 2000.

Lau, D. C. *Tao Te Ching* (bilingual edition), Hong Kong: Chinese University Press, 2001.

Le Guin, Ursula K. *Lao Tzu: Tao Te Ching: A Book About the Way and the Power of the Way*, Boston: Shambhala, 1997.

Legge, James, *Tâo Te Ching by Lao-Tzu*, New York: Dover, 1997.

Lin, Yutang 林語堂. *The Tao Te Ching by Lao Tzu* (http://www.terebess.hu/english/tao/yutang.html#Kap08, 09/26/10).

Lynn, Richard John. *The Classic of the Way and Virtue: A New Translation of the Tao-te ching of Laozi as Interpreted by Wang Bi*, New York: Columbia University Press, 1999.

Mair, Victor H. *Tao Te Ching: The Classic Book of Integrity and the Way*, New York: Bantam, 1990.

Mitchell, Stephen. *Tao Te Ching*, New York: Harper Perennial Classics, 1998.

Morgan, Diane. *Magical Tarot, Mystical Tao: Unlocking the Hidden Power of the Tarot Using the Ancient Secrets of the Tao Te Ching*, New York: St. Martin's, 2003.

Nam, Huai-Jin 南懷瑾. *Lao Tzu Ta Shui* 老子他說, Shanghai: Fudan University Press, 2000.

Palmer, Martin, and Elizabeth Breuilly. *The Book of Chuang Tzu*, New York: Penguin, 1996.

Pine, Red. *Lao-Tzu's Taoteching: With Selected Commentaries of the Past 2000 Years*, Mercury House, San Francisco, 1996.

Sit, Kwan-Yuk C. *The Lord's Prayer: An Eastern Perspective*, Great Barrington, MA: SteinerBooks, 2008.

Smith, Edward Reaugh. *The Burning Bush: Rudolf Steiner, Anthroposophy, and the Holy Scriptures: Terms & Phrases*, Hudson, NY: SteinerBooks, 1997.

Star, Jonathan. *Tao Te Ching: The Definitive Edition*, New York: Tarcher/Penguin, 2003.

Steiner, Rudolf. *The Being of Man and His Future Evolution*, London: Rudolf Steiner Press, 1981.

———. "Calendar of the Soul" (lecture in Cologne, May 7, 1912), *Anthroposophical Quarterly* (London: Anthroposophical Society of Great Britain), spring 1963, vol. 8, no. 1.

———. *Christianity as Mystical Fact: And the Mysteries of Antiquity*, Great Barrington, MA: SteinerBooks, 2006.

———. *The Foundations of Human Experience*, Hudson, NY: Anthroposophic Press, 1996.

———. *Genesis: Secrets of Creation*, London: Rudolf Steiner Press, 2002.

———. *How to Know Higher Worlds: A Modern Path of Initiation*, Hudson, NY: Anthroposophic Press, 1994.

———. *The Influence of Spiritual Beings upon Man*, Hudson, NY: Anthroposophic Press, 1961.

———. *The Influences of Lucifer & Ahriman: Human Responsibility for the Earth* (revised ed.) Hudson, NY: Anthroposophic Press, 1993.

———. *The Mission of the Folk-Souls: In relation to Teutonic Mythology*, London: Rudolf Steiner Press, 2005.

———. *An Outline of Esoteric Science*, Hudson, NY: SteinerBooks, 1997.

———. *The Secret Stream, Christian Rosenkreutz & Rosicrucianism*, Great Barrington, MA: SteinerBooks, 2000.

———. *The Spiritual Hierarchies and the Physical World: Zodiac, Planets, and Cosmos*, Great Barrington, MA: SteinerBooks, 2008.

———. *Theosophy: An Introduction to the Spiritual Processes in Human Life and in the Cosmos*, Hudson, NY: Anthroposophic Press, 1994.

Tam, Bo Gon 谭宝刚, *New Thoughts on the Cultural Meaning of "Taiyi Shengshui"* 《太一生水》文化意蕴新解 (http://www.confucius2000.com/qhjb/tysswhyyxj.htm, 09/26/10).

Waley, Arthur. *The Way and Its Power, Loa Tzu's Tao Te Ching and Its Place in Chinese Thought*, New York: Grove Press, 1958.

Wan, Zhen Huan 尹振环. *Bo She Lao Tzu Shi Xi* 帛書老子釋析, Gui Yang, China: Gui-Zhou Ren Min, 1998.

Watts, Alan. *Tao: The Watercourse Way*, New York: Pantheon, 1975.

Wu, John C. H. *Lao Tzu Tao Te Ching*, Boston: Shambhala, 1990.

INDEX

act with nothing, 95
action-non, 95
akashic (etheric) records,
    31, 161
    as memory of the
        cosmos, 161
animal kingdom, 161–
    162, 165
anthroposophic/
    Anthroposophy,
    vii–ix, 9, 15, 22,
    31, 40, 55, 61, 164,
    171, 174–176
astral, 166
    body, 22, 86, 161–163,
    165
    substitute astral being,
    162
Atlantis, 4
atma, 165. *See also* spirit
    body

bellows, 13–15, 51, 74,
    150
bestowing virtue, 4,
    14–15, 50, 54
Bible writers, as advanced
    seerers in spiritual
    world, 177
bow stretching, 156, 160
breathing, 22
bu (not), 18
Buddha
    Cosmic Buddha, ix
    Gautama Buddha, 57
    nature, ix
buddhi, 165. *See also* life
    spirit
Buddhist, ix, 57

calamities, 20, 26–27, 31,
    99, 107

capital punishment, 151
Castaneda, Carlos, ix
chaos, 169
Chen Cheng-Yih, 4
chien hexagram, 175–176
Chögyam Trunga
    Rinpoche, 57
Christ, ix, 22, 55, 164
    Christ event, 164
    Christ spirit, 165, 167
    as King of kings, 55
    as seed, 165
    as the Son, 167
Christians, ix
Chuang Tzu, xv, 28, 88
clairvoyant, 163
clever/cleverness, 8, 23,
    37, 39, 42, 71, 134
cognition, viii
compassion, viii, xii,
    116, 128, 141–142,
    149–150, 153–154
Confucius/Confucian, x,
    xi, 57
conscience, ix, 39–40,
    117, 150
consciousness, viii, 40,
    45–46, 93, 163–167
consciousness soul, 166
cosmos/cosmic, 23, 163,
    170
    cosmic evolution, 164,
    169
    cosmic sleep, 168
cross, 55

Dalai Lama, 118
    See also Tenzin Gyatso
Dan-Fu, King, 28
death, 91, 104–105, 113,
    141, 149–154, 160,
    163

desires, 3, 5-9, 10, 35, 77,
    102-103, 107–108,
    147, 156
desires no desire, 117,
    132, 135, 147
    as war horses, 99
destiny, 54, 111
dew, 4, 15, 69, 117
Di tribe, 28
divinations, viii, 40,
    82–83
Don Juan, ix
dust, as the world, 11

ego, 95
egoism/egoistic, 23, 102–
    103, 125–126, 140,
    146, 167
elemental spirits, 15
emptying desire, 35
epiphany, personal, 86
ether, 168–169
    air, 168–169
    earth, 168
    life, 169
    light, 168
    sound (chemical),
    168–169
    warmth (fire), 168–169
    water, 168–169, 175
etheric, 162, 169
    body, 23, 61, 161–166
Evolutionary phases
    (epochs), 164–165
    Earth phase, 164–165
    Jupiter's Day (New
        Jupiter), 164–165
    Moon's Day (Old
        Moon), 164–165,
    168
    Saturn's Day (Old
        Saturn), 164, 168

185

Breinigsville, PA USA
20 January 2011
253755BV00001BA/4/P